Tiny Armor?

...grow a suit

Growing God's Armor ...
Stronger than Hell

Doug Dees & Mark Lambert

HIGHERLIFE
PUBLISHING & MARKETING

Tiny Armor? ... grow a suit

Published by HigherLife Development Services Inc.
PO Box 623307
Oviedo, Florida 32762
www.ahigherlife.com

Cover art by Tammy D. Buchanan (tammydbuchanan@gmail.com)

ISBN: 979-8-9899401-0-3 (paperback)
ISBN: 979-8-9899401-1-0 (ebook)

Printed in the United States of America

Contents

Foreword

I have good news and bad news.

First the bad news.

Because of sin in the world and its enormous effects on humankind, there is pain and suffering. We are vulnerable to attacks from satan. You see it all around you and may question why this all happens. It's hard to watch what people can do to each other, and how things like addictions and violence can permanently scar lives.

The short answer to "Why?" is simple.

It's sin.

The sin which began with Adam and Eve's decision to disobey God's simple, specific instructions for life. They chose to believe satan, over God. With that disobedient choice in Genesis they unleashed sin on all of us. (For the grammarians among us, please realize we know that "satan" is a noun and would normally be capitalized. We are intentionally not giving him the respect of capitalizing the name.)

The good news? God knew all we would face. He currently sees all that goes on and has a plan in place to shield you from the worst effects. He gives us a way to have a relationship with Him, and life, and abundant joy during all that happens around us. He has a much larger plan that does away with all the turmoil and pain we see. And for those who know Him, there will eventually be nothing but peace and living in close relationship in pure holiness with Him forever. No sorrow. No tears.

But that's in the future.

For now, He allows choice to play out, and the battles which ensue because of that.

Your choices.

The choices of others.

The effects of both.

If you're exhausted from the battle so far, this book is for you. If you're not sure you have what it takes to do what God is asking of you, this book is for you. If you've ever felt attacked, put down, or pushed back by the enemy— ever sensed that there must be more to the fight than feeling like you never gain ground—or ever felt like the only work you have is the daily grind to hold your own position in this war, this book is for you. If you've been shoved in a corner, and almost willingly given up on life and yourself—if you want not only to stand your ground, but to advance the cause of Christ by setting captives free, this book is for you.

It could be that you've been around the block many times and you've learned some ways to depend on God and have built some armor already. You may want to build it further or learn how to share your shield with others. You may be a strong spiritual leader who helps coordinate the sharing of shields but still want more ideas on how to grow and harden your armor. This book is for you.

However, the enemy will not hesitate to highlight your name on his whiteboards in hell, and up his game against you.

We still have things to accomplish here before our "final" eternity begins. God wants to help us accomplish our part—if we'll let Him, and if we'll follow His leadings. Ephesians 2:10 (NIV) tells us, "For we are God's handiwork, created in Christ Jesus to do good works, which God prepared in advance for us to do."

He knows the afflictions we face and is willing to provide protection from the assaults of satan who wants to undermine who we are as God's children and everything we are trying to do for Him. Our Father has plans for us to counteract what's going on in the world, and in our lives specifically. He wants to help us "grow our suit" of armor with Him, through His Word and prayer, to protect us from all that satan wants to do to us. Remember, "Greater is He that is in you, than he who is in the world" (1 John 4:4 NASB). And this Spirit will empower us to be and do what God has laid out for us, as we build our armor.

In the process we grow closer to our Father. Our armor thickens and strengthens, providing more covering so we can resist more fully. Over time we become even more fruitful and can accomplish more of the Ephesians 2:10 "work" that He has for us. In fact, the more we build, the more God will do through us. As a result, we develop more joy. John 10:10b says, "I came that they may have life and have it abundantly."

One way to think about this book is to blend C.S. Lewis's *Screwtape Letters* with "the message of the arrows" from John Eldredge and Brent Curtis in their book, *The Sacred Romance*. We then delve very deep in how to actually build armor to deal with the onslaught of satan, and to help rescue others. We detail ways to develop that armor from the essentials you get at salvation, to fully blown armor. And how to overlap armor with others so we can protect each other.

You'll find real life examples of the battle, and how the armor works. We can't and shouldn't do this alone. Life is a team sport.

If we don't have a good understanding of our enemy, we won't take seriously our need for armor protection. We won't know how to use this defensive weaponry and also how to push back offensively against the gates of hell. If you think satan's only a guy in a red suit with a pointy tail, or a fallacy like the Easter bunny, you might want to stop.

This book is perhaps not for you. Or maybe it is.

Ask yourself these questions:

- What are the subtle and vicious challenges I face regarding satan? Do I really understand the enemy?
- Can I seriously grasp what it takes to accomplish God's amazing plan for me and my life, and for others?

- How can I develop, grow, and harden my armor so I can not only stand my ground, but also advance the cause of Christ in the rescue of souls?
- Could I really be a part of that? Yes, you can!

The Armor of God

Finally, be strong in the Lord and in the strength of his might. Put on the whole armor of God, that you may be able to stand against the schemes of the devil. For we do not wrestle against flesh and blood, but against the rulers, against the authorities, against the cosmic powers over this present darkness, against the spiritual forces of evil in the heavenly places. Therefore, take up the whole armor of God, that you may be able to withstand in the evil day, and having done all, to stand firm. Stand therefore, having fastened on the belt of truth, and having put on the breastplate of righteousness, and, as shoes for your feet, having put on the readiness given by the gospel of peace. In all circumstances take up the shield of faith, with which you can extinguish all the flaming darts of the evil one; and take the helmet of salvation, and the sword of the Spirit, which is the word of God, praying at all times in the Spirit, with all prayer and supplication. To that end keep alert with all perseverance, making supplication for all the saints, and also for me, that words may be given to me in opening my mouth boldly to proclaim the mystery of the gospel, for which I am an ambassador in chains, that I may declare it boldly, as I ought to speak. (Ephesians 6:10–20)

This Ephesians passage will be our text. We suggest you hide this in your heart. You will need it.

Three clarifying points as we start:

One – *This book is not just for men.* Paul used a warfare armor metaphor to describe some attributes we can have as a result of our connection with God. But the letter to the Ephesian church was not only for men—nor is the armor. The armor of God is for all who follow Christ. And Paul asks us to pray for ALL the saints.

Two – *Some assembly is required.* When you become Christ's, you receive the immense security of your soul being "sealed for the day of redemption" by the Holy Spirit (see Ephesians 4:30). You also receive what armor you need to start the battle. But you do not get handed a fully formed, fully built, or fully functional suit of armor. However, you do get full access to all the armor you want … to grow in each and every area. But you need to start building, and not assume this armor just grows on its own.

Three – *Batteries are not included, because batteries are not needed.* Your strength comes from Christ's might, and the power of His Spirit. The strength to grow your armor in depth and breadth is Him.

Chapter 1

Before the Enemy Was, Christ Is!

...be strong in the Lord and in the strength of his might.

(Ephesians 6:10)

Your strength is in the Lord and in His might, not yours!

Many of us take His strength for granted. Or we do not depend on it at all.

So, before we focus on the enemy and his desire to take you out, we need to firmly establish that you have a way of protection and escape. And it is a highly personal protection. Christ as a close personal friend and covering is the answer.

The unfortunate truth is this: too many of us live with tiny armor. We don't know what it takes to oppose the enemy when needed. Our armor needs developing.

Even as you read these first sentences, some of you are having a knee-jerk reaction. You're thinking, "The armor is God's armor.... You put on that armor and you're armed ... right? God is not weak." That's totally true. He is not weak in any sense of the word. But you are. I am. We are. So, our armor must increase; it must grow. We must put it on ... increasingly.

Deep heart knowledge and mind knowledge of God the Father, God the Son, and God the Holy Spirit must increase and be used increasingly as armor. Christ has secured each piece of armor just for you. You are to grow in it, in Him. You "put on Christ"— His salvation, His truth, His righteousness, His faith, His peace, and you can wield His Word. Each piece must grow. Since Christ has always existed, He will always be the answer to all that you face. But for you to really wear the armor well, it (He) must become personal, not just factual.

> **Armor-building is an ongoing process which should increase until you pass into the next life.**

Armor-building is an ongoing process which should increase until you pass into the next life.

Christ as Covering

How does Paul's illustration of armor help us understand that fact? And why exactly is the enemy shooting at us?

To begin, it is because he hates God and anyone that looks like God—as well as those that don't. He will take out anyone he can using any method he can. But he is specifically targeting anyone that looks like God, anything that is God's, and any group or gathering that might become God's. He shoots at our hearts, our souls, our minds, our strength—

anything he can attack which remotely might serve God. He goes specifically after our strengths to knock us back, and then expose our weaknesses. But he wants to kill our hearts for God. He did it to Eve, and then Adam.

The enemy hates us in ways that can't be explained. We have unbelievable strength available to us in Christ. We are God's highest creation. But in Christ, we have the strength of His might. And that is in the armor of Christ.

The enemy knows that. He also knows we will overuse our natural strength and deny our weaknesses, and we will under-protect both. All because he knows we struggle to know well *whose* we really are, and *who* is there for us. He hates how and where Christ is using you or plans to use you. He hates it all. He hates Christ and anyone who would even think about following Him. Remember, this is the one spiritual being who went up against God and wanted to take His position as creator. (See Isaiah 14:12–14.)

The fact that the "created" wanted to be the "creator" is ludicrous. It's about as crazy as a son telling a father he wants to BE his own father. It's just as crazy as this: if a pecan told a pecan tree that it wanted to *"be the tree it came from,"* the tree would respond by saying, "That's not possible because I created you. You can't be me!" To which the pecan would say, "Well I'm going to get a bunch of my friends and we're going to take over and we're going to be you."

All I'm saying is that's just nuts.

Christ Is for Us

This enemy comes to steal, kill, and destroy. But *Christ* came to give life abundant. But the abundance is Christ *as a person* living in us, not just as one who saves from a distance. He is our way, our truth, and our life. The enemy isn't just trying to wound you; he wants to take you out. All of this seems too jumbled sometimes, too overwhelming to ever know how to fight back. But, the simple answer, the simple truth, is … "be strong in the Lord and in the strength of his might" (Eph. 6:10). Be strong, and continue getting stronger in His might, His armor. It's an ongoing process that builds over time. And the gates of hell will not prevail against what is built by Christ.

The enemy knows where you are strong, even if you don't. He also knows your weaknesses.

> *The enemy knows where you are strong, even if you don't. He also knows your weaknesses.*

If you choose not to have the armor of God on, and not to grow that armor, you are choosing to do just what the enemy wants. That one arrow he shoots, that one sinful habit—you like it. That sin you don't want to let go of, that lie you love to believe because it brings you some false feeling—you like it, and you allow it.

But in the end, the lie will burn up all it can around where it lands. Through the Holy Spirit, your mind is probably already identifying some sins. And I guarantee the enemy will guide you to the old regular ones that everyone identifies. He will let you have that little win. All the while hiding the ones which he does not want you to discover by putting on Christ's armor. The pieces of armor cover you. And they expose your adversary and his ploys.

You may say, "I'm not that bad." No matter where you are on the spectrum of bad, there is always someone worse. Here are a few potential issues. You might say, "I know I am sometimes unkind and want my way too much of the time, but I am almost always right, so it's okay." That's a lie. You might also say, "I realize that porn is not good for me, but just a little and not that often won't hurt, right?" Lie. These are just two of the more useful and obvious ones the enemy uses. He would want you to just try to work on those only, and not delve any further. He will give you some wins in some obvious area. All the while attempting to continuously hide the others which Christ wants to expose and develop armor for.

Christ is waiting on you to approach Him and work on building that suit of armor—made of Him. As that armor grows, it will expose all that the enemy has for you.

In what ways do you think, "I've got this"? Do you use your own might instead of Christ's might? How is that working for you? Do you realize there is work you must do to fully develop your armor? Do you know what that entails? Have you fallen, and are just not sure you can get up?

Again, Christ is available.

And waiting.

When you get knocked down, stand up. With what little strength of His you have, stand up that day. Then stand up the next day when it arrives. Do not take on more than one day at a time, though the enemy wants to heap as many potentially bad tomorrows as he can on you. And he wants to bring as many bad yesterdays to mind as he can to crush your heart today. Don't think about yesterday. Don't worry about tomorrow. Our great Father will give you what you need today. Withstand today. "Therefore do not worry about tomorrow, for tomorrow will worry about itself. Each day has enough trouble of its own" (Matt. 6:34 NIV). He will help you today, and also when tomorrow gets here.

Believing Lies

To be who Christ is, you need to know what you know in your heart, and know it to be true. The enemy can cause you to believe God wrongly. He will cause you to believe wrong things about our Father. Incorrect beliefs. Incomplete beliefs. He will tell you lies and cause you to believe them with all you heart. He would rather you not believe in God at all, but if he cannot get you to avoid believing in God, he will cause your truth to be twisted. He did it with Eve. He won that battle. And Adam just stood there.

I know much about not believing God. I have misunderstood Him in many ways. But He is gracious. God leads me, as He will you, through many paths of misdeeds, misbeliefs, and unwarranted attacks from the enemy.

Eve only got her belief in God a little wrong. She said that God said "…and you must not touch it, or you will die" (Gen. 3:3 NIV). That's a lie. God never said that. The enemy knew she did not know the truth very well. So, the serpent said to the woman, "You will not certainly die" (Gen. 3:4 NIV). Look what happened a few verses later:

> *So when the woman saw that the tree was **good for food**, and that it was a **delight to the eyes**, and that the tree was to be **desired to make one wise**, she took of its fruit and ate, and she also gave some to her husband who was with her, and he ate.*
>
> (Genesis 3:6, emphasis mine)

Believing a lie, she thought, "It's food, it's pretty, and it will make me smart." The enemy landed one arrow in Eve, and then Adam. The human race has been burning ever since. We are all born dead in our trespasses and sin. We are born burning (see Ephesians 2:1), yet Christ is ready to hand us beginning faith (see Ephesians 2:8–9): "For by grace you have been saved through faith. And this is not your own doing; it is the gift of God, not a result of works, so that no one may boast."

The enemy also tried this incorrect believing with Jesus soon after His baptism, while He was in the wilderness.

The enemy lost.

But if that enemy would look at Jesus, the creator of the universe, directly in the eye and say with a straight face, "All this I will give you, if you will bow down and worship me" (Matt. 4:9 NIV), why would he not come after you? How did Jesus respond to this incredible affront? He stated true truth that He firmly believed. He quoted what He knew to be true. Then Jesus said, "Away from me, satan!

For it is written: 'Worship the Lord your God and serve him only'" (Matt. 4:10 NIV).

We hide truth in our heart for Christ to bring it to our mind. "I have stored up your word in my heart, that I might not sin against you" (Psa. 119:11). It's hard to use what is not stored up. And this truth of His existed before satan existed.

Armor must be made of Christ's true truth. You will find highly personal and relational *truth* in His *Word* about *peace* you have because of your *salvation* in Him, and the subsequent *righteousness* you have because of your *belief/ faith* in Him with all your heart. That sentence covers all six pieces of the armor. One truth can be part of all the parts of the armor. All because of Christ! But this is a hard thing to understand.

New Believer – Christ Is in Us

Let's think through why a new believer would need to develop armor, versus having a fully developed, gleaming set of armor at the point of salvation. Think of that event. Someone accepting Christ's gift of salvation changes everything. They now have full access to God. They have the Holy Spirit indwelling them 24/7. They are a new creation according to 2 Corinthians 5:17 (NIV): "Therefore, if anyone is in Christ, the new creation has come: The old has gone, the new is here!"

And their salvation is sealed according to Ephesians 1:13–14:

*In him you also, when you heard the word of truth,
the gospel of your salvation, and believed in him,
were sealed with the promised Holy Spirit, who is
the guarantee of our inheritance until we acquire
possession of it, to the praise of his glory.*

Christ is now in us through the Holy Spirit. This person's salvation is now sealed and impenetrable by satan or anything else. It can never be harmed or taken away or altered.

But would you expect this new believer, on the day after they accepted Christ's free gift, to have a thought life that was one hundred percent completely different from the day before? Yes and no. They now have Christ. But they are still living in their old nature and body, and they still live on a fallen planet with years or decades of past habits and experiences.

Would they have completely different habits and friends the day after this amazing event? Would they have, or demonstrate, any more wisdom or maturity, or have fruit in their lives from one day to the next? Some, but not all. You would not expect earthly perfection the day after salvation. But you would expect them to begin the process of growing in Christ. Our new self is *"being renewed"* after the image of our Creator (see Colossians 3:10). We are a new creation. And some creations seem to be *"being renewed"* more quickly than others. Armor figures into this growth.

That new creature starts to act and think differently about themselves. It is the beginning of a lifelong process of sanctification. It means growing in Christ every day as we follow the promptings of the Holy Spirit. It took me a while to understand that this simply means talking to Him in prayer and learning more about Him through His Word. And being with other believers as we mature. And we will, over time, exhibit Christ in more ways. But it takes time. It takes obedience. It never stops this side of heaven.

All of us who follow Christ are in differing places in this process. You would not expect the new believers to know much Scripture. If they did learn it in Sunday school years earlier, they have a head start. But knowing it is not the same thing as believing it. As

How many of us as Christ followers are walking around wearing more flaming arrows than armor?

they learn Scripture and believe it and fold it into their lives, they are being transformed. You would assume their level of knowledge and belief about Christ would be much smaller early on. So, their armor—which is the outgrowth of this maturing process—would be small and thin. They would be open to many more attacks because they are still thinking some of the same things and believing some of satan's old lies.

Some of you are still at this point. The same as you were the day after your new birth. If you have tiny armor after many years of being a Christian, it's not the Holy Spirit's fault. He has touched your heart many times about talking with Him and reading the words given to us in Scripture to build us up and grow us. We get to listen to His voice, or to ignore it.

That's where our paths diverge.

The journey is up to you.

The Holy Spirit is ready to grow you as fast as you want to. Are you ready?

How many of us as Christ followers are walking around wearing more flaming arrows than armor?

Older Believers

Even as an older Christian, you must build armor. If you have known Christ for twenty years or more, it is also possible that you are not twenty years old in Him, but you have been at "one year's worth of development" for twenty years. If you can't state what you believe, the arrows which are flaming will land right there, and not be extinguished. They land in your spiritual flesh and burn.

Are you more wounded than healed? Do you know Him as the God who heals, and the God who gave His Son so He can be your armor? Are you wearing Him well? I'm afraid many of us are not. But He is our healer, if we will let Him.

You may deal with being anxious at times. Your anxiety will be in direct proportion to the degree that you do not know Him as your peace: the shoes—the sandals of peace. Have you acknowledged that He is your peace? Or do you look for peace in your circumstances or situations? The enemy cannot steal your peace if Christ is your peace.

You may feel alone at times. You do not know Him deeply as the One who never leaves you, never forsakes you. The One who holds you tight, and no one can snatch you from Him or His Father. You may not know that you are sealed by His Holy Spirit all the way to the day of redemption. To

———————————

None of us are handed a fully

developed suit of armor.

We must grow in Christ!

———————————

the degree you know and deeply believe these truths, your shield of belief is being built in that area. You are desiring that "pure spiritual milk" which will cause you to grow into that salvation you have (see 1 Peter 2:2). You need a deep knowledge and faith that you are saved, and can grow the armor of God. What you don't know can harm you!

This all may feel a bit daunting, or a little condemning. It is neither. We hope this wakes you up to the fact that much of this is up to you. You must grow up in Christ or go down in flames. But, when you do grow in Christ, you can rescue others. As you learn how to build armor, you will learn what areas and parts of your shield and your armor are lacking (not lacking in Christ's ability, but lacking in your knowledge and ability to build in that area and use the armor well). If we are to know who He is, we must know what He has said and how to use it to work for His kingdom, and fight for the release of others. You need armor which is thick, wide, and formidable in Him.

Here is what did not happen when you became a follower of Christ. God did not say: "Here's your armor. Some assembly required. Good luck!"

He is with you at every turn, every day, and every moment to help you build the armor, to grow in your faith, your righteous action, and your knowledge of truth. Because Christ IS the armor, as you "put on Christ," you "put on the armor." Coverage grows. And you keep putting on Christ. Put on Christ every day, bigger, better, more complete, increasing in depth and strength.

Christ is *for* you.

Christ is *in* you.

Christ can be increasingly *on* you.

None of us are handed a fully developed suit of armor. We must grow in Christ!

No wonder the enemy hates us. You need God's armor because you have an enemy. And because you have an enemy, you need God's armor. Know that! You can have ultimate protection given from the God of the universe who wants you to be victorious. Christ has you!

In this book, we want to take a slow-motion look at real arrows of the enemy and our real reactions to them in real time. We want to stop long enough to look at life's game films and analyze them, to slow the action down and watch just what is going on. We also want to learn how spiritual armor works, what happens when it is non-existent, how the enemy fashions vicious weapons against us, and how satan's repetitive arrows assault. We want to help you learn how to build your own suit, how to do so continually, and then how to teach others to do the same.

Does God want your armor thick and shiny, or thick and worn?

He wants us to build it and polish it for battle. He wants us to be ready. But as we are in battle the armor will get worn.

What should we do? Keep it polished and it can blind the enemy.

Chapter 2

Born Naked

Put on the whole armor of God....

(EPHESIANS 6:11)

We're all born naked.

No clothes.

We're all born spiritually naked, too.

No spiritual covering.

And satan is shooting at what is spiritually uncovered or barely covered. If you are not yet Christ's, you have no salvation protection, and no armor—none. No spiritual protection.

You have to put something on, because you have nothing on.

We are all in spiritual battles, but you might be fighting your battles naked. Those of us who have chosen to follow Christ have been given the essentials of a suit of spiritual armor. So, to be clear, without out accepting Christ's offer of salvation you are completely spiritually naked, without protection from satan. And you

You have to put something on, because you have nothing on.

have no relationship with a great loving God, who wants that relationship more than anything. If you do follow Christ, you have what essential armor you need to assure you arrive in heaven. But, unless you have been building your armor, you don't have the full growing armor of God.

You have partial coverage.

Think of it like this. Your insurance agent tells you that your car is under-insured. You have liability, low amounts on injury, and nothing on damage to the car itself—whether an accident, or hail, or a tree falling on it. You are covered, just barely. Being partially covered as a follower of Christ is like having little pieces of each part of the armor, just enough to be covered with the basics.

Yes, those pieces are solid enough. Enough salvation to get you into heaven, but not enough for you to know how to "work out your own salvation" (see Philippians 2:12–13). Enough peace to get you through the small issues of life, but not enough peace for large problems or calamity. You have enough truth to believe that God exists, but not enough truth from His Word to know how He will guide you through life. You have what you need, but now you need to grow it. You're still somewhat spiritually naked. In 1 Corinthians 15:53–55, God had Paul write:

> *For this perishable body must **put on** the imperishable, and this mortal body must **put on** immortality. When the perishable **puts** on the imperishable, and the mortal **puts** on immortality, then shall come to pass the saying that is written: "Death is swallowed up in victory." "O death,*

Remember: you get full access

to all the armor you want.

---

where is your victory? O death, where is your sting?" (emphasis mine)

The enemy will not go away quietly. He will shoot his way forward at you, at what, or *who*, you are wearing. We can't wear what we don't know exists.

Remember: you get full access to all the armor you want.

Starting Point

Two important things to remember as you move from naked to armored up:

One – We tend to be able to remember the *names* of the armor pieces, but forget what they *represent*. We tend to remember the illustration and not the point of the illustration. We must know the pieces. More importantly, we must know what they represent—and build them!

Two – Each piece of the armor IS Christ. Each piece represents something He IS, and has done for each of us, and we are to wear it (Him). But we must learn how.

The starting point for armor is accepting Christ's gift of salvation—forgiveness from your sins forever. Saved from a life of separation from God, and being eternally separated from Him because of that same unresolved sin. That's what we are saved *from*. But we are also saved for a life more abundant with Him—here, and then forever in heaven.

That's a pretty sweet deal if you ask me.

We win twice.

At salvation, you get the starter kit. We don't mean to diminish the essentials of armor you receive from Christ because of what He has done. But it is a suit of armor that hopefully you will build upon with Him as you grow spiritually.

Growth is not required. We're not obligated to build upon it. Christ just offers it, and we should accept the offer.

Many people, however, choose not to grow a suit. You too can actually just keep your tiny suit of armor, and have little spiritual coverage beyond the essentials. You are still going to heaven when you die. But you'll be allowing yourself to be beaten almost senseless until then. It is not required of you that you grow your armor. It's just smart if you do. When I think of a starter kit of armor in my mind's eye, I see an adult wearing a toddler-sized Iron Man costume to a Halloween party. They get into the party, but it just doesn't fit right, or cover very much.

Christ must increase; you must decrease.

Now, don't get me wrong. The suit you get at salvation is enough to get the Spirit living inside you, and genuine entrance into heaven. That is if you truly said to Christ, "I believe that You are who You say You are." After all, the thief on the cross did not have much time to build a suit. What He did have was Christ. Christ told him so while hanging right there next to him. So, when that thief got to heaven, and let's say that proverbial question from God happens … where He says, "Why should I let you into My heaven?"…

the only thing that thief can say is, "The guy on the cross next to me said I could come in, and I believed Him."

Christ must increase; you must decrease.

In 2 Peter 1:3–11, the apostle outlines that the qualities of Christ in (and on) us must increase. If that does not happen, you will remain nearsighted, vulnerable, unfruitful, and ineffective. To the degree Christ does not increase, you will be pounded upon by the enemy where you are vulnerable ... and with tiny armor, that is pretty much everywhere. Just know that if you don't grow, the arrows will hit with much more impact and destruction. You may well get *singed* over and over, or seriously wounded because you are believing the devil's lies and not protecting yourself with who God is.

The promises He has made to you are personal and wearable. As you believe and wear that truth He wrote in His Word, you build strong, thick, deep armor. God is not like your mom when you were two years old. He is not going to dress you. He gifts you enough to start. It is up to you, with Him, to increasingly put on the armor consistently, thicker, stronger, and it will swallow up the sting of death.

Paul writes further saying, "The sting of death is sin, and the power of sin is the law. But thanks be to God, who gives us the victory through our Lord Jesus Christ" (1 Cor. 15:56–57). When we allow arrows to land in our spiritual flesh, it is the sting of death: sin. We believe the enemy and not God. The enemy will then use the world against us. We will do what we can to soothe the wounds on our own. We will use what we can grasp from the world and the flesh, as the devil orchestrates our putting on anything besides God.

There are many aorist active verbs in this "armor or God" passage. In English we have verbs which are past, present, and future. The aorist type verb does not really exist in the English language. It has no real time designation. It basically can represent past, present, and future. It has no real regard to completeness, duration, or repetition. And, in this passage, there are also a lot of participles … words which end in "-ing." So, if you have accepted Christ's gift, you have "put on Christ," are "putting on Christ," and should "be putting on Christ." Yesterday, today, and tomorrow. It covers all three. Continually, increasingly, "putting on" Christ.

This armor of God IS Jesus. His salvation. His peace. His truth. His righteousness. His faith. His Word. Jesus IS the armor.

Christ has done His unfathomable part to secure all these for you. Do not take His offered gift lightly. You must do your part. Increasingly wear it, and build it, with Him walking you through life by His Spirit. He has begun a good work in you, and He will continue it (see Philippians 1:6). You don't have to take the enemy's onslaught just standing there. Preparing is imperative. Building this armor ahead of time is necessary.

We cannot follow the world and follow God at the same time. The desires of flesh are against the Spirit, and vice versa (see Galatians 5:17). Many adults who say they follow Christ, do not realize they have been walking around with tiny armor, half-dressed. They may be following the flesh, not the Spirit.

We can actually rest in Him, with armor on. But we can't decide to relax and not wear our armor. You can't sit down in armor. Are you fleshly thinking that you will feel over-dressed? What if no one else is wearing armor (metaphorically)? What if they believe differently than you and act differently because of it? Will wearing armor cause you to stick out? Let's hope so.

Parental Covering

Those of us who have disciples as parents, or grandparents and mentors, have had somewhat of a covering as they have raised us and led us. Their prayers and examples guided us. But we must decide on our own. Do we accept the gift Christ offers? Will we develop the armor He gives us?

At our physical birth, our spiritual father was the enemy. But when we believe, and have accepted Christ's offer, His gift, and have turned from what we formerly believed toward Him, and said we believe Him, we are saved. "Because if you confess with your mouth that Jesus is Lord and believe in your heart that God raised him from the dead, you will be saved. For with the heart one believes and is justified, and with the mouth one confesses and is saved" (Rom. 10:9–10).

So, then we have a new dad, God the Father. We are now related. However, the enemy does not give up what rights he thinks he has on us when we are adopted into a new family, the family of God. Our adoption is so certain that we are actually no longer related to the enemy. We go from being related to him, to being related to God through Jesus Christ.

Think about this: your name is now in the Book of Life, written there by Jesus. But your name is also on a "whiteboard in hell," and the enemy will do what he can to steal, kill, and destroy anything in your life that even smells like the aroma of Christ. He wants to take you out. You are now in the fight of your life. He does not want your soul making a difference in the world. He wants you mostly naked and hunkered down in a corner hoping the storm will be over soon. The enemy is like a bad dad coming after the kids even after adoption has happened. But God has a restraining order on him, and God will be your new dad, teaching you how to grow well.

After the covering was lost in the garden … we were all born spiritually naked … or dead in our trespasses and sins (see Ephesians 2:1). We need salvation and covering. Christ is both! We do not get a glorious life handed to us. It is a joyous fight to the end as we move toward glory. I say joyous, because we now have a loving Father who will give us everything it takes to win. But we have been duped into believing that God does not love us and has left us to fend off the enemy on our own. It is the enemy himself who has convinced us of that.

Spiritually Hypnotized

You may have been hypnotized by the enemy. You are comfortable and have cleared out a nice little spot for yourself. You want to think you are covered enough, but in your heart, you know you're not.

You're not drawing near to God.

You're not making any difference in the lives of others.

You don't have the power of Christ in your life.

You may think, "I go to Sunday school every Sunday. I pay my tithe." You may even sing in the choir. You may dust your hands off and say, "There, I've done my part. What else is there?"

If the enemy has you that comfortable, are you really engaged in the war going on around us? There is no doubt that he's probably struck you with a flaming arrow that anesthetizes you into thinking that your job is done. You're comfortable, standing still as the battle goes on around you.

You will not win the battles you do not fight.

In all circumstances, every single day, the enemy will do all he can to stop you from moving forward. He never takes a day off. He may start by suggesting that you believe you are a pretty strong team member because of the list you checked off above. In fact, God's lucky to have you on His team, isn't He? Do you see the hypnotic traps? And it can start with good things. But as you sit there proudly wearing your attendance medal you are not engaged.

You will not win the battles you do not fight.

If the enemy has you standing there flat-footed, comfortable, and anesthetized, you are believing a lie of flaming arrows. He has you standing still. So, he may leave you there frozen for a bit, but he will be back sooner or later. Will you wake up and build armor?

Why Armor?

In your mind, as well as in your actions, you need armor. You must engage in the battle or you will be taken out slowly. Pushed back. Minimized. Stolen from. Destroyed.

This armor covering was not completed in some assembly line and handed to you fully and completely assembled. But, remember, you did get the starter kit. If you truly believe in your heart Christ is who He said He is, you have salvation (the helmet), are righteous in God's eyes (the breastplate), and beginning faith (the shield), which are all part of His truth (the belt). So, you're in, but are only somewhat covered for the battles of life. You have something to build on now!

Armor is vital. How else would men who went before us, like Dietrich Bonhoeffer, be able to stay faithful? His armor was built and he was wearing it. He was sober-minded, and the enemy was looking to devour him. Dietrich was executed on April 9, 1945. But his writings live on to spur us on! But can we say: God is my God; what can man to do me? They may take my life, but they cannot take my soul. Christ's stance in front of us (as we wear Him), and our faith in Him, and love for Him, is what an onlooking world needs to see.

We see examples of men and women of incredible faith and stamina from God for kingdom work. And then we catch ourselves getting upset at a missed parking place. I think the biggest reason for that is this: we have tiny armor. They have built theirs but we have not.

Let me tell you a short story. I was talking with a man who was not a follower of Christ. He and his wife had attended two different types of church on and off over the last twenty-nine years. They came to our church, and at one point he said to me, "You guys are always talking about Jesus." To which I replied, "Jesus is a pretty big deal around here."

In the conversation that followed, it became obvious that they had never accepted the gift Christ offers. They had not chosen to follow Him. They were not His. They knew about Him, but they had not become His.

Then the next week, the man said, "I feel like I have been beaten up since I was five years old."

I held that thought and came back to it a bit later. I said, "Do you want to know why you have felt beaten up since you were five? You have no armor."

They both stared at me with question marks on their faces.

I told them to open the Bible they had with them and read Ephesians 6:10–20. They did that silently together, then looked back up at me. The looks on their faces were priceless. "What the heck is all that about? Armor?"

I said, "No wonder you've felt beaten up since you were five. The enemy has had a clean shot any time he wanted. You have been running around spiritually naked for your whole life! You have been pummeled by flaming arrows from the enemy for all these years. You need to grow in Christ."

Thankfully this couple did believe who Christ is in their hearts, and now follow Him as Lord of their lives. They are now building their armor.

You can grow up in Christ or lie face down in flames.

Armor Is Only an Illustration

As we have said, armor is an illustration used by Paul. But I'm afraid we get stuck on the illustration and lose the meaning behind each piece of the armor. It is not like an exoskeleton, like Iron Man. It is more like a spiritual plating which increasingly holds up your soul internally and externally as you fight spiritual battles. Granted, Paul's illustration is a great one. But we must understand how each piece represents a deeply spiritual relational offer from God Himself, and not get caught up on the parts of the illustration. We must see how each part can cover our spiritual nakedness.

> **We do not get handed a perfectly formed suit of armor at the moment of salvation.**

We do not get handed a perfectly formed suit of armor at the moment of salvation.

———————

You can grow up in Christ or

lie face down in flames.

———————

But, we do get a seal of ownership. Remember, we are "sealed for the day of redemption" (Eph. 4:30). I believe that. I also believe there are many folks who think they got their "Go-to-heaven ticket" punched because someone had them just say a prayer. But they didn't really mean it.

Words were said, but their heart was not involved.

That was years ago, but nothing has changed in their lives.

Still completely naked. They took it as some incantation. I am sure that wasn't the intent of the person who asked them to pray. But, for the one who prayed that, let me say this to you: you can talk to Jesus right now and mean it in your heart. You can respond to His offer of forgiveness and allow Him to become the One who runs your life. Talk to Him now. Come be on our side. I pray you do! Then get ready to build your armor and prepare for a battle.

It's the only way to get the armor in the first place. The enemy does not like that we pray, and that we talk to Jesus. That is an understatement.

Important side note: you really need to talk to a more mature believer, a follower of Christ, who you know in a local church who will help you move forward as you grow in your faith. Wandering alone in life without others is an impossible battle to win. You will get taken out. You need others! This is a team sport. Paul ends this passage with prayer for himself and all the saints. You have the protec-

We have to know our armor and grow into our armor.

tion of others who are building their armor, too. Without it, you're lunch for the worst predator of all time.

> *We have to know our armor and grow into our armor.*

For those of us who have known Christ for a while, including me, we may not have known how to develop or wear the armor. It remained an illustration for years. It was new knowledge to me when I realized that each piece should change and grow in its understanding, intensity, and usage.

- Jesus IS our salvation.
- Jesus IS who we believe and have faith in.
- Jesus IS our righteousness.
- Jesus IS truth.
- Jesus IS peace.
- Jesus IS the Word made flesh—and all pieces increase.
- Jesus IS our covering and our example, and all parts of the armor of God for us.

How well do we know the parts? How deeply do we believe them? How often do we grow in what we know? I'm afraid that most of us have tepid answers for these questions.

There Has Always Been a Need for Armor

In the Old Testament, when you read about David as he goes out to face Goliath, he is offered another man's armor. It's just too big and doesn't fit. So, he goes with what he's accustomed to, a slingshot and five smooth stones. The armor he was handed was man's armor.

He turned that offer down.

What he went out to fight with was God's protective armor.

David knew he had a spiritual covering. He knew God was his shield. He said, "You come to me with a sword and with a spear and with a javelin, but I come to you in the name of the LORD of hosts, the God of the armies of Israel, whom you have defied" (1 Sam. 17:45). *David's shield was the Lord of hosts.* God had prepared him for that time. David later said, "You are my hiding place and my shield; I hope in your word" (Psa. 119:114).

Gideon was a fearful farmer hiding in a winepress while threshing wheat. But God called him "O mighty man of valor," and turned him into a mighty warrior (Judg. 6:11–14). Did you notice in that passage that the angel says "you" and Gideon says "us"?

It had not hit Gideon yet that the angel was talking about him, not just a general group. We too tend to focus on what can be done in large groups. But God speaks to each of us through His Spirit. "But, as it is written, 'What no eye has **If your faith is small, your ability to fight those battles will be, too.** seen, nor ear heard, nor the heart of man imagined, what God has prepared for those who love him'—these things God has revealed to us through the Spirit" (1 Cor. 2:9–13).

If your faith is small, your ability to fight those battles will be, too.

The Old Testament is full of men and women who went into battle with the Lord's covering. They knew that the battle is the Lord's! He is who goes before us. He is our fortress (see Psalm 59:9). He is our shield (see Psalm 33:20).

Joshua led Israel in the battle of Jericho. It was a different battle in the way they won. The Lord went before them. Yet Joshua and Israel lost the next battle. But it was because of the sin of Israel (see Joshua 7:11). David won many battles. At one point David did not go to battle, but the enemy worked at taking him out by using Bathsheba to draw him into sin. David would have never seen her if he had been out with his army.

Deborah fought when others would not move forward (see Judges 4). The Lord was willing to step in front of them back then. He will also step in front of the arrows for temporal onslaught against your soul. If you have armor on, then as you move forward, the Lord IS in front of you, and goes before you.

We have many disciples who went before us to show us how. They are our witnesses to tell us how life goes when you go with Christ. And He was and is our great example.

> *Therefore, since we are surrounded by such a great cloud of witnesses, let us throw off everything that hinders and the sin that so easily entangles. And let us run with perseverance the race marked out for us, fixing our eyes on Jesus, the pioneer and perfecter of faith. For the joy set before him he endured the cross, scorning its shame, and sat down at the right hand of the throne of God.*
>
> *(HEBREWS 12:1–2 NIV)*

You need armor just as the men of old did. Think about it. If your faith is small and you are in battle, it may seem like you are holding a Tupperware lid as your shield of faith. How many flaming arrows are you going to extinguish with that? Tiny armor just won't do. Your faith must be strong and wide, and thick, and ready to extinguish the flaming arrows of the enemy.

God knows that.

Do you?

Or do you go out unprepared and hope for the best?

How big is your faith? What is your faith made of? Your sword of the spirit may look more like a pickle spear. And your faith shield may be more like a Tupperware lid. You are fighting battles which are not tiny.

There will be losses. More losses than need be. In Mark 9:19, there is the man who had a son possessed by demons since childhood. The demons had caused him to convulse horribly for years. The man asked Jesus to heal his son, and at one point he says, "Help my unbelief." He knows his faith is small. The word used here is the opposite of faith. He says, "Help my un-faithfulness. Help me where I don't believe. Help me to have more belief." In Greek, the same word is used for "belief" and "faith" depending on whether it is a noun or a verb. Is your faith a verb? Is it active and growing? Christ is the "perfecter of our faith" (Heb. 12:2).

> *Don't go into battle with a Tupperware shield and pickle spear!*

———————

Don't go into battle with a

Tupperware shield

and pickle spear!

———————

Search God's heart and His Word and find how you can have all parts of the armor necessary, and growing, to fight the battles He has for you. There is joy in the wearing, and in the results of wearing it. He IS the suit of armor. His attributes are love, joy, peace, patience, kindness, goodness, gentleness, and self-control. When you get the armor, you get Him.

Reduced Exposure

Christ is asking us to reduce the areas that the armor doesn't cover. We realize our armor is built from the belief in our heart. As we said, the heart is where it starts. Reducing the exposure for arrow strikes requires making larger armor. A smaller exposure because of larger and stronger armor. Reducing exposure can also happen by being close to someone who has more developed armor. Pretty ingenious. Less visible spiritual flesh, and more armor.

Are the pieces you wear big enough for the battles you fight?

It's one thing to feel like you have a real need because you had an arrow almost get through. It's another to feel like you should make the armor broader and stronger even if that last arrow bounced off and got extinguished. Don't rely only on the first original piece you got at salvation. Instead of tiny armor, you need bigger, thicker armor. And, as you will see, there are different gauges of steel available.

Are the pieces you wear big enough for the battles you fight?

Consider "heart"—that word comes first almost every time in the Bible—before "mind." Too much of the time we start with "mind" and stay there, never attaching our heart. And that's a problem. It is with the heart you believe (see Romans 10:9–10). As you will see, the enemy wants you holed up in a lightless house with no connection with the world. He wants you pushed back and shivering at the thought of facing him and life. But, it is as simple as holding your shield up, and moving beyond where you are, all the while knowing you belong to Christ as you go into battle.

Standing Your Ground

I am certainly not invincible by any means, but I am learning how to stand my ground. I feel free to ask God how to take the next step forward, how to lock down the armor I have as much as I can, and how I can stand firm as I build more.

In the Scripture passage about God's armor, He states that we are to:

- stand against
- withstand in the evil day
- stand firm, and
- stand therefore.

We will get into this more deeply later. But think about this now—as you build your armor, the enemy is required to respect that armor. The same word for "withstand" that is used here, is used in James 4:7: "*Resist* the devil and he will flee" (emphasis mine). How is that possible? He is fleeing Jesus, not you. It is Christ ON you and IN you that he is fleeing. The enemy has to flee.

At this moment you may be thinking, "I'm not sure I have ever noticed the enemy fleeing from me or Christ in me. I'm not sure I could ever imagine that being the case in my life." But it's God's armor you are building, not yours.

The enemy of the universe has got to be ticked since he has to flee from us tiny humans. But it is Christ, the armor of God, which does that.

It must be humiliating to satan. But do we believe that? Jesus gave the twelve apostles power to heal and cast out demons. Whether or not you believe that disciples today have that same power is up to you. But this armor is for every follower—every follower. But you must build it up in Christ (see Luke 9:1, 6). As we move forward, our armor faces forward. God is your "rear guard." "For you shall not go out in haste, and you shall not go in flight, for the LORD will go before you, and the God of Israel will be your rear guard" (Isa. 52:12). So, God has your back.

When the Arrows Do Pierce Your Flesh

Many arrows will land. Your spiritual flesh will burn like you can't imagine. But you already know that. You know your failings. You know your mental and emotional tendencies. You know the wrong things you run to, which you think will satisfy life. You know when arrows land, big and small—if you are honest. And yet you may be numb to the landing of these flaming arrows. In your spiritual nakedness you may have been hit so many times, it feels like that is the norm. Just how things are. But deep in your soul, deep in your heart, you know that is not true.

There could be victory, and arrows could flame out on the other side of your shield. So, before we get to all that, I want to say, God heals where the arrows land. He is always there. He is Jehovah Rapha, the God who heals. "He heals the brokenhearted and binds up their wounds" (Psa. 147:3). "When the righteous cry for help, the LORD hears and delivers them out of all their troubles. The LORD is near to the brokenhearted and saves the crushed in spirit" (Psa. 34:17–18).

Never forget, God heals where the arrows land.

You are righteous.

You are His.

You have that promise from Him.

If you are not His, you will continue to burn. But, He's only a prayer away. Yet for many, they just will not believe He exists and is who He says He is. For them, the burning is for now, and for eternity. It does not get better, only worse. If this is you, I beg you to reconsider who you think God is. His might comes with

> **Never forget, God heals where the arrows land.**

knowing truly who He is and dismissing the lies you used to believe. satan knows the big picture, and that the victory is already ours. But that victory is not always manifested around us every day. Yet, if we look, we can see Christ at work, in battle. Will we build our armor and go out, or hide?

He never called us to worry and wring our hands. In fact, on about 295 occasions He says do not worry, or fear, or fret, "for I am with you" (Isa. 41:10). So, you either believe that's true or you don't. If you're wringing your hands and worrying about the state of the world, you don't believe what He says. You're lying to yourself.

If you belong to Christ, you will not experience hell eternally, though you may succumb to some of hell's influences here on earth. How many believers do you know who have stopped following Him well? Have you had those moments, too? Build some armor, and be strong in His might. The enemy is afoot.

You will not get the armor built by the end of this book. It takes a lifetime to assemble a covering of armor, and a great deal of intentionality to draw closer to Him. But you must start and you must continue with steadfast determination. Over time, you will build it.

Don't try to fight naked. You will lose. Remember, the suit is not fully developed, but the materials are fully available.

Chapter 3

The Enemy – Who He Is, Who He Is Not

Put on the whole armor of God, that you may be able to stand against the schemes of the devil. For we do not wrestle against flesh and blood, but against the rulers, against the authorities, against the cosmic powers over this present darkness, against the spiritual forces of evil in the heavenly places.

(EPHESIANS 6:11–12)

Through Paul, God described who we are up against before He addressed the armor we need to grow into. We too will examine the enemy first before talking about the armor of God. Don't get bogged down by our discussion of the enemy. We hate to give the enemy this much content, but we must. You should not take lightly who he is and who his henchmen are.

It is vitally important to dispel what you think about the enemy. We need to expose the depth of his subtle and viciously wicked desire to take you out. It's also crucial that you do not dismiss issues in your life as merely circumstantial or that negative circumstances are just the way things are. Life now is not as God intends forever. The enemy existed long before creation and rebelled. Because of that rebellion, you and I are under fire in ways we can't imagine. So, we will imagine a better future for all of us.

As Christ's followers, we have God's part and our part, our different responsibilities. He shields you, but you too must shield you. In 1 Peter 1:4, He describes our salvation as our "inheritance that is imperishable, undefiled, and unfading," which is shielded for eternity. But we have a responsibility to build armor (of Him) to also shield ourselves now. As you read about the enemy, ask yourself, "Has he done any of this to me? What does he do that am I not aware of?" And, "How have I been able to respond? Where do I need to grow some armor?"

The three reasons we need armor are our world, our flesh, and the enemy. We were born fallen and we were born with an enemy. But God is gracious enough to give us His armor to protect us.

An easy way to remember what the Bible means by "flesh" is by an acronym: FLESH—Following Long Established Sinful Habits. But, GRACE (God's Riches At Christ's Expense) gets us what we need for armor. As we grow up, we establish habits we don't even know about. We develop ways of dealing with life. We don't know arrows are flying from the enemy. But we all do know about pain, disappointment, tragedy, and a list of horrendous things that can and do happen to us when we are younger.

Flaming arrows have been landing which some of us don't even know about. We have developed ways of talking to ourselves and we believe ingrained lies. As we grew into adulthood, we developed methods of coping that accommodate our pain.

But now, whatever your age, you need to know that you can have armor to protect you, and that this available armor will heal you because the armor is a person. You and I also need to know who the enemy is and what he is up to. You need to know that though he and his henchmen cannot be everywhere all the time, they can set up traps in the world to affect us and cause our flesh to desire wrongly. Not to give the enemy more than he is due: he is due nothing but punishment forever. But we're addressing who he is. Why?

> **satan will stop at nothing to try to make you completely ineffective.**

So you will know what the armor is for.

So that you do not mistake him for a caricature and think of him lightly.

Christ doesn't.

The following is to make certain you realize you are not fighting a red-suited, cartoonish caricature of the real satan. This enemy is subtle, deceiving, shrewd, wickedly cunning ... and a murdering liar. He and his henchmen are the most evil and vile beings that exist. There are no words to truly describe the vicious way he will attack. He is like a roaring lion, ready to shred your spiritual and physical flesh in any way possible. He detests the fact that you are alive and hates every breath you take as a child of God.

satan will stop at nothing to try to make you completely ineffective.

But don't forget, in John 10:10–11, Jesus tells us that "the thief comes only to steal and kill and destroy. *I came that they may have life and have it abundantly. I am the good shepherd*" (emphasis mine). In heaven there is no armor because there will be no need for it. In fact, we will be with the good Shepherd, the One who is our armor. As you read through this chapter, remember, as followers of Christ, we can stand firm in His strength, not our own. But here, we must build our suit of armor—made of Him.

Anything evil is from the enemy, the thief, the liar. We have to recognize the evil effects of the flesh in our lives, which are not satan himself, but are used by satan, caused by satan, and engineered by satan within this fallen world. So, the world, the flesh, and the devil are against us. He has methods which go beyond our comprehension.

Again, God describes our enemies four ways—we are up against formidable spiritual rulers, authorities, cosmic powers, and spiritual forces. This enemy will use whatever he can to destroy anything of God … His creation, His will, His people. You. Me. No one is safe from his reach here on this planet even though God only allows him a short reach. We will talk more about that later. But for now, suffice it to say, evil is against you and will be until you die. But you *can* overcome evil because of Christ.

satan is smarter than you alone. He knew the Word before the Word became flesh.

---

satan is smarter than you alone.

He knew the Word before the

Word became flesh.

In 1 Peter 5:8, we see that satan prowls around *like* a roaring lion. satan is a liar and always has been. He is not a lion. Christ is the roaring lion. Christ is the Lion of Judah. Christ is Aslan in C.S. Lewis's *The Chronicles of Narnia*. The enemy is nothing like Christ. He is the absolute opposite of Christ. His power is not comparable to that of Christ. But his powers are not something you should go up against on your own. That is why you and I need the armor of God, each piece of which represents a major attribute of who Jesus Christ is and what He has to offer you.

> *The enemy acts like a lion. But Jesus Christ is the Lion of Judah.*

In the next section we'll talk about the whiteboard in hell with your name written at the top. We think this image fits how the enemy works, and how insidious, pervasive, predatory, and scheming the enemy is. Below your name on that whiteboard are some of the things satan thinks God has planned for you. The enemy does not know all of God's plans. Only God knows all that He has planned. The enemy can tell what is going on by observing your life, your actions, and reactions. God also knows everything written on that whiteboard in hell. He knows how satan will attempt to defeat you. God knows this fallen angel better than satan knows himself and better than he knows anything or anyone.

The enemy may know your actions, but God knows what's on your tongue before you say it, according to Psalm 139. He knows every aspect of every battle from all sides, and He knows everything in advance. He allows choice to play out because choice gives us the ability to choose to love Him on our own rather than from His coercion. By the way, that's why God doesn't always stop bad things from happening to people. He gave us a real choice in the garden to follow Him, and we didn't take Him up on it. Now we get the chance to choose what or who we will follow. The enemy wants to take out everyone on the planet and take them with him to hell.

No wonder the world has had so many problems since the fall. And it continues. Does it seem like the world is more divided than ever? Does strife seem to be the order of the day? It says something when we actually notice that things are not going well in many areas. The enemy loves divi-

> **The enemy acts like a lion. But Jesus Christ is the Lion of Judah.**

sion, anxiety, chaos, and confusion. What we might have missed is that there has always been spiritual warfare going on around us all the time since the garden. Only now do we notice it. And the enemy does not just create all this disorder randomly. He makes it personal. He is after you as well as me.

Again, in 1 Peter 5:8–10 (NIV), we are reminded to be alert and sober-minded, to stand firm, and that we are not alone:

> *Be alert and of sober mind. Your enemy the devil prowls around like a roaring lion looking for someone to devour. Resist him, standing firm in the faith, because you know that the family of believers throughout the world is undergoing the*

same kind of sufferings. And the God of all grace, who called you to his eternal glory in Christ, after you have suffered a little while, will himself restore you and make you strong, firm and steadfast.

Do You See the Enemy Properly?

Even amid the things we see today, when you mention satan or the devil you can quickly get some knee-jerk responses. For many, satan is in the same category as the tooth fairy and the Easter Bunny. He's a cute little caricature of a guy in a red suit with a spiky tail and red pitchfork. He's a little myth believed by people who are afraid of the boogeyman. Others are at the other extreme. They are so under the pile, oppression from satan blocks out God's voice, and they have no hope because satan seems to be in total control. He seems stronger than the impact of God in their lives. All is lost. Both extremes are very dangerous. satan would love for us to see him as a simple, benign caricature. Someone who has no intentions of hurting us, because, after all, what did we do to him? Or he wants you to see him as being everywhere and in control of everything. It's just not so.

There are others who see this battle as a prize fight. Two fighters, nose to nose in an equally matched fight. That also couldn't be farther from the truth. God is far superior to satan, far more than can be imagined. This enemy is a being, created by God, who fell because he wanted to be like God and to be God. To this day he hasn't given up on that vision. As the verse above says, he is *like* a roaring lion seeking whom he may devour.

He hates you and your soul and will do literally anything to make sure you fail and feel defeated. He would love for you to be like those who feel so overwhelmed they can't hear God's voice. In the 1960s, a comedian named Flip Wilson had a recurring skit where he ended the story by saying, "The devil made me do it." It was funny, but not good theology. satan can't make you do anything. But he can tempt you and try to pile on when life is not going well. His strategies are myriad. But you get to choose your response.

So, Who Exactly Is satan?

He is called one of the most beautiful angels in all of heaven. Lucifer, who became satan, was beautiful and wise and was appointed, as an angel, to be the guardian cherub (see Ezekiel 28:11–15).

He did not fall from heaven; he was pushed.

God had to cast him out because unrighteousness was found in him. This ex-angel is now running hell with the one third of God's angels who were cast out along with him. His beauty and wisdom may be the reason he started to see himself as competition for the throne of God. He said he wanted to be equal to God. That's when evil started. That evil was not extended to humankind until Adam and Eve sinned by listening to and acting on what satan was telling them—that they too could be like God, and that's why God didn't want them to eat the fruit of that one tree. They fell for satan's story and ate the fruit they were told not to eat. He didn't tell them the full story, that his desire to be God got him cast out of heaven.

That fruit-biting incident is when evil migrated to us, and we fell from our uninterrupted relationship with God. Because of their decision, Adam and Eve were cast out of the garden. It was easier for satan to talk to them than ever before. They now had evil in common. It has been that way ever since.

> satan is a lyin' lion. He roams around like a lion. He will tell you things that aren't true in the hope that you will believe them.

Since he was the second most powerful angel who lived in heaven, he is more powerful than you on your own. He is quicker than you. And he is ahead of you. If satan can talk one third of the angels out of heaven, he can talk you into hell. Right now, he is being held back from doing all that he wants, which is to take everyone out and take over. He will never get to do that, but he will never stop trying. But you are not on your own.

Who satan Is Not

I don't mean to make him sound more menacing than he is because he has none of the "**omnis**" that God has.

He Is Not Omniscient

satan is not all-knowing.

He doesn't know all that God knows about you. He can't read your mind, but he can see patterns of behavior that he can use in the future to try to trip you up. He doesn't play by any rules. He makes this evil up as he goes. I'm reminded of the scene in *Pirates of the Caribbean* when Johnny Depp's character, Captain Jack Sparrow, a pirate, is having a sword fight with Orlando Bloom's character, Will Turner. Sparrow picks up some dirt and throws it in Turner's face. Turner is offended that someone would fight that way. He says, "That's not how gentlemen sword fight." Sparrow points at his own chest and says, incredulously, "Pirate."[1] In essence, what would you expect from him, a pirate?

satan is a lyin' lion. He roams around like a lion. He will tell you things that aren't true in the hope that you will believe them.

Pirates don't follow many rules. They will do anything it takes to win, even if that means cheating.

So, when you think of satan, think "pirate." He's satan—what would you expect? If you think he won't bother you when something bad has already happened in your life, you misunderstand his nature. If you are lying on the ground in pain, you are much more susceptible to everything else he can hit you with. He only cares about your destruction, and he doesn't care how that happens.

satan knows he can also use something good to trip you up. That's fair game to him. If you're on three different committees at your church, that may be a good thing. But

---

1   Verbinski, Gore, dir. 2003. Pirates of the Caribbean: The Curse of the Black Pearl. Buena Vista Pictures Distribution, California. 143 minutes.

if it means you aren't around your family much as a result, he will use that to sow destruction in your family, in your marriage, and with your kids. They may wonder why Mom or Dad cares about everyone else but them. You can put your family on a pedestal too. Ask many pastor and missionary kids if satan doesn't use good things to bring about division and destruction.

satan does not get to define how you walk this life. He has no "omnis." God does.

You may say that doesn't seem fair. If you're trying to advance the kingdom, shouldn't there be a rule that protects you because you're trying to do good things? Sorry, that's not how that works: "Pirate."

satan does not get to define how you walk this life. He has no "omnis." God does.

He Is Not Omnipresent

satan is not everywhere at one time.

He will use things that are bad, as well as good, to get you to question your faith and most often the goodness of God.

He is confined to certain areas. God has temporarily given satan some power over the world per 1 John 5:19: "We know that we are from God, and the whole world lies in the power of the evil one." And in Ephesians 2:1–2: "And you were dead in the trespasses and sins in which you once walked, following the course of this world, following the prince of the power of the air, the spirit that is now at work in the sons of disobedience." He will do what he can where he is to get you to question your faith and most often the goodness of God: "How could a loving God allow that to happen to me? Am I not really a Christian, or is God not powerful enough to help His servant? Or does God just not care enough to help me?" Have you ever had these questions?

The pain and suffering we see around us is part of the fall, and through human sin satan has been given some control over the earth for a season. That sounds menacing. But it's not unlimited power. He cannot be everywhere at once.

He will use things that are bad, as well as good, to get you to question your faith and most often the goodness of God.

He Is Not Omnipotent

satan is not all-powerful.

He is limited in his abilities. Even though he has been given some ability to intervene in our lives, he can only do so from a distance. He doesn't get to do anything to us that God doesn't first see. So that means God allows bad things to happen to people, right? Nope. That happens because we fell, and we now live among fallen people making fallen choices. God does not cause bad things to happen to people. If God doesn't stop it, He is either not all-powerful or He doesn't care—which is it? That's a false choice. God never promised to save us from the effects of the fall in this life. He does have a plan to redeem the world from the effects of the fall eternally, but that's at the end of time, not now.

> *We walk* through *the valley of the shadow of death.*

You may think the devil is everywhere, understands all your weaknesses, and knows everything about you and has free rein to ruin your life. He wishes he could do all that, but he has not been granted those abilities. That doesn't mean he won't try everything possible to make you fall. But he is limited by God in what he can do, and you are offered a chance to build armor to stop it. There is even less he can do against Christians. If you belong to Christ, you are less vulnerable than non-Christians who do not have the Holy Spirit living in them. Job understood the need for God to be who you run to. You need protection. You need armor because this enemy has a whiteboard in hell with your name on it. Job's whiteboard did not end up as satan had designed, even though he endured much pain and suffering.

We walk through the valley of the shadow of death.

You can allow satan to define your life. You can cower in a corner. You can be fearful to the point of being frozen in your steps. But perfect love casts out all fear according to 1 John 4:18. Yes, this world is a fallen world, and satan is the prince of the power of the air, but our King is Jesus. So, do you cower to a fallen prince or kneel to a reigning King?

Chapter 4

The Enemy –
His Whiteboard in Hell

*Put on the whole armor of God, that you may be
able to stand against the schemes of the devil.*

(EPHESIANS 6:11)

I magine one of those large, white, dry erase boards, and
at the top is your name scrawled in black marker. On
the rest of the board is the strategy that outlines the
things the enemy, satan, and his demons, plans for you today, tomorrow, and the day after. There are titles and assignments. If the attack feels very up close and personal, it
is. In case you're wondering why such long chapters on the
enemy—we are both convinced that most Christians have
a cartoon idea of who satan is and are mostly unaware of
his daily assaults, and write it off as just living in a fallen
world. When you think that way, he wins the day.

So, as you read this extended metaphor about the enemy's
conniving evil schemes, ask yourself, "Have I experienced
any of this, and am I dismissing much of it as just life on
this planet?" Though satan and these demons are limited,
and can't always be after you, they still have assignments.
They have an evil, organized, explicit strategy for each of
us involving multiple tactics—and they will shift to whatever works best on each of us.

There is no linear explanation of how the enemy will come after us. But he does. Attacks can be based on what they see we have planned for the day, or on what they think God has planned for us. The enemy knows you better than you know you. He and his henchmen will repeat attacks which worked in your past. They will use whatever works at the moment. Since these tactics don't seem to be linear, you can't prepare for any specific onslaught. But, you can prepare by focusing on Christ and building armor. We'll discuss how to do that in the next chapter.

There's a box, metaphorically speaking, in the upper right-hand corner of that whiteboard with lessons they've learned about you. It contains key strategies the enemy has gathered over time. If you're tired, or worried about money, or whatever vulnerability is unique to you—they have written these down to see which ones can be used in today's assignments. I imagine this box much like the buttons on an old jukebox.

The enemy has numbers for things they know that work on you when you are_____ (fill in the blank):

- alone,
- discouraged,
- tired,
- out of town,
- going through a divorce,
- worried about your relationships,
- money,
- or whatever pushes your buttons.

Let's say button P3 is a good go-to move that still works on you. They will stick with the golden oldies because you still haven't addressed that issue or built a belief shield to repel that arrow. You're still vulnerable to a P3 or D9. If it has even a small chance of working on you, they will use it. We all have different issues unique to each of us. They have observed which ones still work. Clichéd but true—they are always pushing your buttons. And they use arrows to push them. They are also paying attention to potential new buttons that can be developed.

As you are imagining a whiteboard in a conference room in hell you may think it's filled with filthy, no-count slugs living in squalid conditions. You may envision a dimly lit room with old pizza boxes strewn all over the tables and chairs, maybe even the floor, with half-eaten pieces of pizza used to stub out old cigarettes. You might envision old, mostly empty whiskey bottles lying on their sides dripping liquor every now and then. You may smell the stench of overflowing cigarette ashtrays and stale cigar smoke that fills the dingy curtains hanging lifelessly askew on their rods. You might imagine demons still passed out on the couch from the graveyard shift several hours ago.

We're making this up, but it might not be like that. Hell may be spotless, well lit, with modern conference rooms, and the whiteboards are connected to a state-of-the-art system that translates the scribbling on the board into a master computer. This computer might compile inputs for the day into a tracking system that feeds a master scheduling system. Then, maybe, this compiled information is sent to top leaders. His ways are an insidious business. They are prob-

---

Don't just stand there getting

pummeled.... If you're not

fighting, you're losing ground.

---

ably equipped with the latest technology to manage the overall operation. After all, he is called the prince of the power of the air in Ephesians 2:2. I've always wondered if that meant airwaves. I'm sure there are metrics kept about success rates for each day and tracked by week and year to see if they are improving in their use of these black arts on us. While the specific details about this conference room may be made up, the spiritual battle it represents is very real. It is not fictitious or a caricature. The spiritual warfare we face each day is incredibly real, and in real time. It's happening now, all around us, every day we're alive.

Don't just stand there getting pummeled.... If you're not fighting, you're losing ground.

In case you think this is only a few conference rooms, just turn around and walk to the doorway. You'll see long halls that stretch in all directions as far as the eye can see. Down the halls are the endless rows of other conference rooms. There is standard wicked work done there. They all do it with the same intent, finding infinite ways to get to the end result. Ephesians 6 describes it as the devil's "evil schemes." The Greek word is *methodias*. He has many methods:

- He distracts.
- He detains.
- He entangles.
- He attempts to re-imprison.
- He desires to steal, kill, and destroy.

He will affect the mind, the will, and any emotion he can get his hands on. The methods are endless. If you venture down other halls, you may come upon a massive control room, like the one at NASA, with huge screens of activity and teams that monitor situations around the world.

The two of us can imagine all these things because we are old enough to have had so very many of his flaming arrows land and sizzle in our metaphorical flesh. We've fought against thoughts, situations, evil from others ... even from those I personally thought were friends. Many times, early on in my life, I wondered why I struggled so much in certain areas, while other Christians seemed to have it all under control. It turned out that some were putting on a good face, as though they were dealing with nothing harsh in life. Looking back, I can see those lies. I know they lied because the enemy was using what worked on me. I didn't know I was wearing tiny armor. It never crossed my mind until I was past fifty years of age. I spent so much of my Christ-following life with undersized armor. I just did not see satan for who he was and what he was up to back then.

The enemy wants to influence what you think in the deep recesses of your heart.

Organization and Strategy

Impacting our hearts and minds is what this sprawling complex is all about. The arrows are aimed at our heart, our souls, our minds, and our strengths. Anything we might use to love God and draw near to Him. Again, there are no rules here. satan will do whatever it takes to shoot lying messages at us that penetrate deeply. If someone loses their mother unexpectedly, an alert goes out to send troops to that spot as soon as possible: "We have an opening, and we need to get there as soon as possible." It's not to console the adult children whose mother has suddenly died, but to perpetrate a lie. To ensure they think that the pain is unjust and caused by a God who has no regard for the tumult in their lives. Troops are sent to guarantee one of the toughest days of their lives is even tougher. Now's the time to pile on the guilt of them not calling their elderly mom the night before to say goodnight. The henchmen of the enemy will remind each one of them about the missed birthday party because they were working late. They'll bring up childhood memories of when they said unkind things to a mom who was only trying to help. They just wanted to do it their way. Lies. Memories. Reminders. The enemy will use anything that will make any situation more painful so that he can kill, steal, and destroy. He will give someone a flat tire or take advantage of her child being sick to overstress their ability to cope with another fresh tragedy.

The enemy will work to have the most negative impact he can.

Have you ever heard of anything like this happening?

Yes. All the time.

I just went through some of that with my dad's passing. The enemy heaps on guilt where he can. But our family has pushed back against him. I'm not saying we didn't grieve. We did! But the grief of missing someone and the secure knowledge that Dad is in the compassionate hands of our amazing Savior are two completely different things!

The enemy wants to influence what you think in the deep recesses of your heart.

The enemy wants us to feel horrendous guilt and be filled with self-condemning thoughts. He will try to direct our heart with our thoughts. But we can "take captive every thought to make it obedient to Christ" (2 Cor. 10:5 NIV). The enemy will hit us in what we might not have done well, even if we tried. Matthew 15:9 says, "For out of the heart come evil thoughts." When that happens, it is our old heart directed by the enemy's thoughts that we did not take captive. My mind is directed by my heart. But how does my heart direct my mind? The truth of what God has said is in Hebrews 4:12: "For the word of God is living and active, sharper than any two-edged sword, piercing to the division of soul and of spirit, of joints and of marrow, and discerning the thoughts and intentions of the heart." And our loving Father, our God, has given us "a new heart" in place of a "heart of stone" (see Ezekiel 36:26). So, let's use that new heart against the arrows and stand firm against the devil.

Whether they are the arrows which are in mass for the masses or the arrows and lies designed specifically for you … they are designed to distract you, disturb you, or take you out. The enemy is incredibly cunning, and so many people don't realize the insidious impact of what's happening. They think, "Hey, it's just a little 'edgy entertainment' I'm watching. I've had a tough day. I deserve a little mental break." Or, one glass of wine, or two, or more. What about meds? Whatever it takes to feel a little better. But these behaviors can have long-term implications. Or maybe it's the pride that comes when you feel you have been successful where others have not. This enemy may work at keeping you from thinking that turning to Christ may be the answer. Again, I know this. We both do, because both of us have failed to build armor well in the past.

Mass Media, Social Media, and Entertainment

If you step further down the hall, you might see enormous film studios with backdrops and sets for movies and television shows providing entertainment for millions. If the enemy can control the content of this media, they can help shape hearts and minds with the things they want people to dwell on. Our society is literally wired to connect to all these outlets for "entertainment" of every stripe. In fact, you realize there is a massive set of industries who do nothing but develop this kind of content. We know that. There are more connections created all the time to tie every device into one central viewing area. It becomes a symphony of content choreographed to entertain but at the same time instill the values that it does. It's insidious to us, the consumer, because we think we are just taking a break from our day. Just kick back and enjoy life with friends or family. It's not a spiritual thing; it's just a way to forget the day and relax a little.

Surely there is nothing going on behind the scenes to affect the hearts and minds of the people watching and listening to all this. It's a respite that they look forward to. But be on guard. The word "media" sounds innocuous, doesn't it? After all, *Mary Poppins* is part of our media. But other words and visuals carry harm. It's just entertainment, right? But it will influence what you call right and wrong. And it will cause you to develop spindly armor when it becomes what develops or informs your belief system.

Even porn can start with seemingly innocuous images. It may be an image that's racy but not really that bad. Maybe it's just an image which tantalizes at first. The problem is that these images progress to other images in the mind. There are millions of people, yes, women too, who have become trapped by pornography on all levels, even just romance novels, either as escape or comparison. Neither works out well.

In the midst of all this media, and social media, what are you thinking about? How does what you consume affect your heart, your mind, your actions? It all does. There are arrows behind much if not all of it. Growing your armor will help you discern how to keep the arrows from landing, how to not let it all in. The enemy will use visuals to create the vilest thoughts imaginable and then condemn you for having them. Christ's armor can stop these attacks.

Personal Tapes (Recordings)

Memories—there is a key element called "personal media" hidden in the back, in a dimly lit area. It specializes in making nothing but personal recordings filled with satan's lies. Recordings, files, however they're played, are for us to carry around in our heads so that we play them over and over in our minds. Deep in our souls we house the hurts, scars, and wounds from a past that we've accumulated over time. It's the memory of someone close to you who said, "You are inferior because...." We all have these memories, tapes that play in our minds that we can't seem to delete. But with God's help, we can turn down the volume so low that we can barely hear it anymore. The process is tough, but not impossible.

Those tapes can haunt us night and day, audio or video. Or they may go years or decades without playing. Sometimes, the tape plays three times a day, or a hundred times. It's satan's go-to move. He spots some scar from your past and keeps that wound open by playing that tape because he knows it's a weak spot for you. Only you, the enemy, and God know exactly what's on those tapes. Unfortunately, some of us have tapes playing we really aren't aware of. Even better for satan, because we don't realize they are playing. So, when the media department sends out that activation signal for a particular tape, it plays and we freeze because we are caught off guard with something from the past that we can't even identify, or choose not to. God wants to help us deal with those tapes, if we'll let Him. New armor can shut down old, bad memories.

Deleting tapes may seem to be impossible. Even as I write, the enemy plays recordings I haven't heard in years. He brings to mind visual memories I have not thought about in decades, all with the hope of distracting, disturbing, or derailing the activity and work God has for me to do.

The metaphorical studios mentioned above are alive with the activity of henchmen. Dozens of departments have afternoon project updates, and they will show who is meeting their schedule and who is behind. And a meeting with the big guy is not the way you want to end the afternoon. You think your earthly boss doesn't have any people skills: try having satan as your boss.

The way the enemy crafts each story for each person is based on each person's past. So many recordings of statements were made for me in my early years. He just keeps hitting play. This tactic is one the enemy uses often on me. They are made up of memorable moments or words spoken to me while I was growing up and as a young man. Like when I was on the playground getting picked last for team. Many of us have that video replayed over the years—implying that we again will not be picked at work for the promotion. The words, "You just can't get it right!" Or, "What's wrong with you?" implying you did not fit in because of what you did or said. How about this one— someone says, "I guess I'll have to do it myself." Meaning you didn't get it done well enough. Teachers, coaches, parents, team captains, friends, and people you don't even know land verbal and visible blows which go not only in our memory bank, but also the enemy's. He will use those arrows again and again and again until you have armor to deflect them. There is a great God who will help you build strong, thick armor made of Him, to withstand these taped assaults.

After my father's passing, the enemy took the opportunity during that great time of grief to bring back some horrible things I did years ago as a young man. These images were completely unrelated to my grief. The enemy will shoot at you any time he can. One thing I have learned—if there are people in these images, I immediately start to pray for them, whomever they are. A girl I wronged ... pray immediately. Somebody I was a jerk to ... pray immediately for him. satan hates that. And as I pray and resist and withstand, the enemy flees just like James 4:7 says he will.

Humor

One of satan's strategies is to make the arrows and onslaught funny. If they're funny, they might seem innocuous. Evil sounds better when it's funny. Whether they're mass media or personal relationships, humor can be used against us. If satan can find people we like, the enemy will use them as mouthpieces for his content. The enemy can always slowly change our standards over time so that what used to be seen as unclean and filthy will now seem normal because we've seen it so much.

In Philippians 4:8 (NIV), Paul says, "Finally, brothers and sisters, whatever is true, whatever is noble, whatever is right, whatever is pure, whatever is lovely, whatever is admirable—if anything is excellent or praiseworthy—think about such things." satan makes sure the content used doesn't appear to be that over the top. He will use anything to convince us that "it's not that bad." Innocuous arrows that create a slow moral drift in your heart and mind to call something "pure" which is not.

The enemy's objective is not just to use media, personal recordings, and humor. The same is true of all the other offices down these enormous halls. There are sound stages where music is made in lush studios with world class musicians. This content exists to change our purpose from God's to satan's. The "social media" department injects ideas and watches trends and adjusts accordingly to make sure the truth is hard to tell from other content. They know that if they can obscure the truth so it sounds enough like the truth, that people will pass it on as truth, and they have done their job. There are ideas for amusement parks and schools—those are a great place to sell false truth. Or an arts department that deals with all the arts, visual and performing, can all work on your downfall. But, there's armor available for that.

satan would love to take something you see as innocuous and entrap you with it.

Lest you think life is all bad news about the enemy, you need to know that the chapter on "Sharing a Shield" will shed a lot of light on the fact that while the enemy meets to discuss and plan our demise, we meet to fend off the attacks and plan rescue missions. The enemy should not be the only ones meeting with intent.

Back to the Conference Room for Regrouping

The enemy will use all these tactics and strategies to kill your soul and to push back any life within you. They will regroup and reassess what is working and what is not.

They will plan new attacks and new strategies. But the conference rooms can get messy when, just as soon as the whiteboard marks are dry on their plans, someone they are attacking reads Romans 8:28 (NIV): "And we know that in all things God works for the good of those who love him, who have been called according to his purpose." And just that quickly a piece of armor pops up and some of the enemy's best plans get twisted into good things. It takes a lot of that liquid cleaning spray to remove all the ink from the board used every day. That aroma stinks to them. It reminds them that God will always one-up them. God somehow twists satan's own twists and can use it all for good. But we have to belong to God for that to happen.

If you are Christ's and you are called according to His purpose, then build some armor and prove that you are.

Choose to grow up in Christ against all of satan's onslaught.

Cumulative Effects

In some cases, the activities can in themselves seem innocuous, even wholesome. Some attacks or arrows will not feel like they are intended to harm.

> *satan would love to take something you see as innocuous and entrap you with it.*

I have some smart, creative friends who after years of using beer to relax have fallen into the trap of thinking that they just aren't themselves without enough beer to take away the pain of the day. They aren't concerned about getting buzzed or drunk. It's relaxation, after all, and don't we all need that? They have become trapped mentally and physically because they have believed a lie. They are funny and fun to be around when they are sober. But they now don't see it that way. Remember, satan would love to take something you see as innocuous and entrap you with it. It could even be good things like work or hobbies. Work is a good thing—how could that become bad?

This is one of satan's go-to moves—taking something that seems good and slowly turning it into an addiction of some sort.

The enemy will use any means he can for you to talk yourself into letting a small ritual develop naturally over time and cause a much bigger problem. He can't take your salvation away, but he wants to do whatever he can to make you ineffective so you're no threat to his kingdom.

The enemy's wiles are so polished and glamorized that they burn images into our brains and hearts, and there doesn't seem to be a delete button. Big arrows, little arrows, innocuous attacks, blatant affronts—they all mark the walls of our soul and heart. And in our brain, they set off a complex set of chemical functions so that we have trouble understanding even a subtle addiction. As with almost everything, he is looking to find anything that will entrap you to keep you distracted. And if you're distracted

This is one of satan's go-to moves—taking something that seems good and slowly turning it into an addiction of some sort.

enough, you may over time wander into sins and allow arrows to land which you would have never considered earlier in your journey when you were convinced it wasn't really that bad. Over time it grows. What was tantalizing at first now requires more to achieve the same effect. That phenomenon is common to all addictions, even things we don't call addictions.

Cumulative Fallout

Eventually, if you resist the pull of the Holy Spirit, who is tapping hard on your heart to walk away from that activity, you may wander into a public sin. That sin will impact your reputation, your family, and your future. How many ministers have crossed that line never realizing that when it became public the body of Christ would be bruised because of their failure to withstand the enemy? They never intended that to happen. There were ample warning signs, and the Holy Spirit was doing His job to point out the folly of the activity, but they listened to the enemy. They welcomed the arrows. Are these saints destined for hell for what they did? No, they are as saved as the day they accepted Christ's forgiveness for their sins. But they didn't live their lives as if they were, and the sober consequences caught up to them, just as Scripture says it will for all of us. Numbers 32:23b says you can "be sure that your sin will find you out." Fallout from the arrows landing will become obvious.

Is it worse when ministers fail in a public forum? Yes, because these failures discredit Christ's name. But, is it bad for regular Christians to fail the same way? Absolutely.

There are people in your life watching you that you aren't aware of. People who know you are a Christian, which makes you an ambassador of Christ, for better or worse. Your impact on them is real. They may not see your arrows land, but they see their effects. The impact on your family and friends will also be there. For the last few decades my wife and I have attended an annual event with her old Baptist college group that meets just to stay in touch. Over the years, a few couples divorced. What do you think then happens to the group? They are genuinely welcomed by all the members because they are friends who love each other and have for decades. You see where this is going.

Typically, neither of them shows up anymore. The awkwardness of being around people who knew them as a couple, they think, makes the situation awkward for everyone else. So, they don't attend. The members of the group deeply miss both of them and tell them so. And everyone misses out on some fellowship and closeness. No one said they weren't welcome. How quickly decades-long friendships can evaporate over something like a divorce. Arrows land and fallout happens. Is the enemy after your marriage? Of course he is. Anything that might honor God is a target for his arrows. You need armor, both of you.

Distracted means you're not paying attention to what God has for you ... and that's good enough for satan.

Would satan take advantage of something like this? You bet he would, because now neither attends the couples' Sunday school class or small home group for the same reason.

Now, time with in-laws for the holidays are out, too. Those relationships built in to their lives to draw them together now draw them apart. It is a favorite move for satan to use events to isolate people from the support they would normally find in their families, their friends, and their church activities. If he can get them out of the herd, they are much more vulnerable. A small change in someone's life can impact the trajectory of the rest of it. They are not going to lose heaven, but their days here will be diminished as they struggle to get back to something that feels normal. Cumulative fallout becomes cumulative distractions.

The bottom line is that this doesn't have to happen. The arrows don't have to land on you.

It is not what God wants for you.

It is not what God intends for you.

But the one *roaring like a lion* is always stalking to see if there are ways to cause you to trip yourself up. It can happen because of something you don't think is a problem. It can happen because you have moved away from God gradually and haven't been responding to His spiritual taps on the shoulder to avoid certain thoughts or activities. It can happen to any of us. So, we must grow an armor made of Him.

> *Distracted means you're not paying attention to what God has for you ... and that's good enough for satan.*

You can still choose to listen to His Spirit, who wants you to grow and to help you develop stronger armor. You can stop right now and change. There are ways to proactively lean into God's prodding. If they are His prodding, you can bet they are what will make you stronger, more agile, and more useful in the kingdom. You will be more fruitful for His kingdom and those around you. You have a lot to do with this process. It's your choice. As the old saying goes, "If you feel far from God, guess who moved?"

Don't Give satan Too Much Credit

It rains on the just and unjust. In a fallen world there are effects that are indirectly from satan. Not everything that happens to you is satan's direct activity, so don't give him too much credit. But it does look to us as if the effects of the conference rooms and media suites are having an effect in our world today. Second Timothy 3:2–5 (NIV) says:

> *People will be lovers of themselves, lovers of money, boastful, proud, abusive, disobedient to their parents, ungrateful, unholy, without love, unforgiving, slanderous, without self-control, brutal, not lovers of the good, treacherous, rash, conceited, lovers of pleasure rather than lovers of God—having a form of godliness but denying its power. Have nothing to do with such people.*

Have you seen any of this around you?

But God has not left you without defense. Since our struggle is not against flesh and blood, but against the rulers, the rebellious angels who are now in authority with the powers of this dark world, we are up against the spiritual forces of evil. But that means there aren't just whiteboards in hell, but also in heaven—the "armor design supplementary section." Heavenly realms means God's kingdom, for Psalm 91:11–12 (NIV) says, "For he will command his angels concerning you to guard you in all your ways; they will lift you up in their hands, so that you will not strike your foot against a stone." In Exodus, Moses covers this topic: "See, I am sending an angel ahead of you to guard you along the way and to bring you to the place I have prepared" (Exod. 23:20 NIV). "Are not all angels ministering spirits sent to serve those who will inherit salvation?" (Heb. 1:14). First Corinthians 6:19 assures us of the indwelling of the Holy Spirit: "Or do you not know that your body is a temple of the Holy Spirit who is in you, whom you have from God? You are not your own."

He is doing His part. Are you doing yours? If you are Christ's, you have the Holy Spirit residing in you all the time. The God of the universe dwells within you, and He will guard you and heal you as you build your armor. The good news is that God desires to be personally involved in every area of your life. His conference rooms, now and in the future, are areas of genuine comfort, relief, care, redemption, protection, and deep friendships beyond what can be imagined. They are all available because of what Christ has done and will do for us. In the end, Christ completely obliterates all the enemy's conference rooms, whiteboards, and the long halls and ops rooms.

You are not in this alone.... Before the enemy was, Christ is! Make certain Christ is your covering!

Chapter 5

Salvation Helmet

...and take the helmet of salvation....

(EPHESIANS 6:17)

If you write a book, somewhere you have to define your terms. Let's start with salvation. There are tons of definitions out there about salvation. It seems to me that they fall into two categories. One is a way of being saved from danger, loss, or harm.

The other is more about the Christian religion. That the salvation of a person has to do with the state of being saved from evil and its effects by Christ's death and resurrection.

I looked at those for a while, and of course you would think the obvious one is the second one about faith in Christ. And that's certainly accurate. But after looking at the first definition I thought, "It's that, too." Preservation or deliverance from harm, ruin, or loss also applies. If I escape hell and separation from God, that's a lot of harm, ruin, and loss I am delivered from. And the synonyms for this definition apply, too—lifeline, preservation—not so much conservation, but means of escape. All of those apply, too.

Salvation all starts with Christ. Everything you receive from those definitions are because of Him and His willingness to set aside heaven, come to earth, and die on your behalf and then get resurrected. God Himself came here for you. The enemy of course will tell you that is not true. But it is true. The enemy will say you do not deserve it. But we are deserving because Christ says we are. It is His choice to offer salvation to us. Salvation is His.

Without salvation, no other parts of the armor exist!

That salvation helmet is not actually your helmet. It is Christ's helmet. He has purchased it and given it to each of us personally. But you have to do something with that helmet. You have to "*work out* your own salvation with fear and trembling, for it is God who works in you, both to will and to work for his good pleasure" (Phil. 2:12–13, emphasis mine). The words

Without salvation, no other parts of the armor exist!

"work out" take on the simple meaning of working at a task. They are used in agriculture and in the making of materials. It is as though God has given you a farm, and you are to work the farm. If you say you are a farmer, you prove it by farming. If you are a saved person, you act like a saved person … increasingly. If you have said Jesus is your Lord, you act as though Jesus is your Lord … increasingly. Your salvation is refined by constant use.

What is our particular part in this process? At salvation we receive all of the Holy Spirit. But at that point He doesn't have all of you—Christ gets more of you over time, but only if you lean in. That's what He wants. And believe me, it's what you want, too. Put the helmet on. Wear it in public. That is your part. Lean in to Him. Abide in Him, for He says, "Apart from me, you can do nothing" (John 15:5). He wants to help you look more like Himself, to think and act more like Him. You want that because that's how you can operate consistently with how He made you. Mark Twain said, "The two most important days in your life are the day you are born and the day you understand why."[2] I choose to consider these words from a spiritual perspective. As we grow to think and act more like Christ, we become more of who He originally made us to be. Even in a fallen world that impacts us and those around us, we can change for the better.

In Ephesians 5:18, God had Paul say, "And do not get drunk with wine, for that is debauchery, but be filled with the Spirit." The Greek word for "filled" can also mean "controlled." Wine can control you, but Paul is saying to let the Spirit control you. Again, at salvation we get all of Him, but He does not get all of us. Over our whole lives we are working out our salvation so that He has more and more of us. It is sort of like a garden hose. It just lays there until the spigot is turned on; then the water controls the hose.

But who wants to be a garden hose?

A firefighter's hose is controlled much more by the water coursing through it. We should be more and more controlled by the Holy Spirit over time. He will help you work

---

2 "A Quote by Mark Twain," Goodreads, 2023. https://www.goodreads.com/quotes/505050-the-two-most-important-days-in-your-life-are-the.

It's not actually *your* helmet—

it's *Christ's* helmet.

He gives it to you.

---

out your salvation helmet and build the rest of your armor over time.

It's not actually your helmet—it's Christ's helmet. He gives it to you.

God explains that the helmet is the first gift He gives us, and it is by His amazing grace that we are saved.

> *For by grace you have been **saved through faith**.*
> *And this is not your own doing; it is the gift of*
> *God, not a result of works, so that no one may*
> *boast. For we are his workmanship, created in*
> *Christ Jesus for good works, which God prepared*
> *beforehand, that we should walk in them.*
> (*EPHESIANS 2:8–10, EMPHASIS MINE*)

The helmet of salvation is given because He loves us. A free gift, from Him, purchased by His Son. There are many days I can't get over that. Why pick me? Why was it offered to me? Because He loves me. And He loves you, too. Do you believe that? The faith to believe is a gift not by works. Yet He does have works for us to do after salvation because we are His. Our works with Him once we are His show that we are His.

You can't lose your helmet, but you can misplace it or not utilize it to the fullest. You have to have it to work it out. If you do not have a helmet of salvation, then doing good things will not earn you a helmet. It is Christ's to give you. There are those who think works will get them a helmet and will get them into heaven. That is a lie from the enemy. Matthew 7:21–23 says:

*Not everyone who says to me, "Lord, Lord," will
enter the kingdom of heaven, but the one who
does the will of my Father who is in heaven. On
that day many will say to me, "Lord, Lord, did we
not prophesy in your name, and cast out demons
in your name, and do many mighty works in your
name?" And then will I declare to them, "I never
knew you; depart from me, you workers of law-
lessness."*

Mark and I are privileged to be a part of a ministry called
G300. It is a group of mission-minded men who support
a ministry called "Little Ones
Ministries," which serves mission outposts in rough areas
of Central America and the
Caribbean. We have a yearly
dinner where each man involved is given a piece of armor.
The first year, they get a real, seven-pound helmet of armor. I must admit it looks awesome when you put it on.
The reason we start with the helmet in G300 is to ensure
every man who receives one knows what it is about. We do
not want any man thinking that any of his good works as a
G300 man will earn him a place in heaven.

**We work because
we *are* His, not
to *become* His.**

Our works as G300 men are out of thankfulness and obedience to Jesus and our genuine love for others. Works without faith will not get you into heaven. But "just as the body
without the spirit is dead, so also faith without works is
dead" (Jas. 2:26 NASB). Works will never earn you salvation. But your works as a child of God will show that you
have salvation.

We work because we are His, not to become His.

This salvation is a heart issue. Romans 10:10 says, "For with the heart one believes and is justified, and with the mouth one confesses and is saved." So, the helmet of salvation is God's first gift to us as armor, given to us because of the faith He extended and the faith we accepted. The helmet of salvation is the daily, moment-by-moment reminder that we are His. Your surety of you being His and He being yours.

The helmet must be firmly fixed, or you will not be able to build any other piece of armor. The enemy will tell you that you do not really belong to Christ. You really did not turn your life over to Him. The enemy will do all he can to get you to doubt your salvation. If he can cause doubt, he can stall the building process. In Ephesians 6:17, "take" means "reaction to action on the other side." In other words, by your reaction to what God has done you receive the gift. You take the helmet. He is reminding you to take the helmet and not forget you have it.

What are the elements of salvation that you wear? When someone gets saved, what does that actually mean? I know the definition we started with, but what is the substance of this armor-plated helmet we get? When you got saved, what did you think it meant? What makes it solid?

Christ died for your sins … past, present, and future. You no longer bear the guilt and shame. Christ defeated death so you don't have to. You won't be separated from God. You are justified because of Christ. You will go to heaven when you die because of Christ. You cannot lose the gift of salvation. The Holy Spirit comes to live inside you … to teach you, to remind you, to guide you. Propitiation has happened—God's wrath toward your sin is appeased. You now have the righteousness of Christ. The Spirit secures your entrance into heaven on the day of your final redemption. You have been reconciled to God, which is the restoration of peace between you and Him. And you begin to follow Christ as a disciple, all because of Him.

We have all sinned, "for all have sinned and fall short of the glory of God, and are justified by his grace as a gift, through the redemption that is in Christ Jesus, whom God put forward as a propitiation by his blood, to be received by faith" (Rom. 3:23–25). Christ came back from death: "God raised him up, loosing the pangs of death, because it was not possible for him to be held by it" (Acts 2:24). Furthermore:

> *We know that Christ, being raised from the dead, will never die again; death no longer has dominion over him. For the death he died he died to sin, once for all, but the life he lives he lives to God. You also must consider yourselves dead to sin and alive to God in Christ Jesus.*
>
> *(ROMANS 6:9–11)*

We're also encouraged: "And do not grieve the Holy Spirit of God, by whom you were sealed for the day of redemption" (Eph. 4:30). And then reminded:

> *I give them eternal life, and they will never perish, and no one will snatch them out of my hand. My Father, who has given them to me, is greater than*

all, and no one is able to snatch them out of the
Father's hand. I and the Father are one.

(JOHN 10:28–30)

You are saved.

You are being saved.

And you will be saved.

God has done all the work of salvation in your life. You either believe that, you do not believe, or you are in the process of wrestling with it. God is the one who sent Christ. God is the one who prepared the Passover Lamb. God is the one who gave the gift you did not earn. God is the one who chose to look at you until you looked at Him to make sure you saw what He had to offer. That is a whole lot of security!

You are saved, you are being saved, and you will
be saved. Saved increasingly.

You may say, "I know this. I hear it every Sunday morning." Great! Are you working it out in your own life? Others of you may be saying, "I'm not sure what I believe about this salvation thing." Then we would suggest this— stop reading this book and go get one or both of these two books: *The Case for Christ* by Lee Strobel, or *Evidence That Demands a Verdict* by Josh McDowell. These two books are excellent, and we cannot,

> **You are saved, you are being saved, and you will be saved. Saved increasingly.**

nor do we need to, try to explain it better. These two men have done that exceedingly well.

Chapter 6

Belief Shield

In all circumstances take up the shield of faith,
with which you can extinguish all the flaming
darts of the evil one.

(EPHESIANS 6:16)

I f you don't get these next few chapters, failure to extinguish flaming arrows is certain.

On Days You Don't Fight, satan Wins

As said earlier, we are part of G300 men. My friend, Mike
Denton, envisioned a group of men ready and on mission
here—and there. They are on the "mission field" in their
own walks in life, and collectively helping to establish
twenty-five mission points in the "mission field" out there:
Central America. The Caribbean. These men are called
G300 because they are named after the three hundred men
who went with Gideon and took out the enemy.

Gideon said to the angel, "Please, my lord, if the LORD is
with us, why then has all this happened to us? And where
are all his wonderful deeds that our fathers recounted to
us, saying, 'Did not the LORD bring us up from Egypt?'"
(Judg. 6:13). Gideon asks a good question. They are fear-

———————

The enemy wins every day you

don't go out to fight.

———————

ful. They are doing their work in private. Getting on with life, threshing wheat in a winepress so the enemy won't find them. That was Gideon before God called him out.

The enemy wins every day you don't go out to fight.

satan does not win the war. We know that. In the words of the old gospel group, the Cathedrals, "I've read the back of the book and we win."[3]

But we're still in the game. Think about it as the fourth quarter. At times it can feel out of control, like we're losing. We see fumbles or losses on the field and wring our hands. We can lose perspective about the big picture—that the victory is already ours, but it is not always manifested around us every day. Yet, if we look, we can see Him at work, in the battle. Will we go out, in all circumstances, or will we hide?

He never called us to worry and wring our hands. In fact, on about 290-plus occasions, He says do not worry—or fear, or fret—because He is with us. So, you either believe that's true or you don't. If you're wringing your hands and worrying about the state of the world, you don't believe what He says. You may say, "Well, I really do. I just don't show it sometimes." Right. That means you really don't believe it. You're lying to yourself. satan loves it when you do that. It saves him a trip, and some arrows. However, he will show up if he thinks he can steal a day or a month or

---

3   The Cathedrals. "I've Read the Back of the Book." The Cathedral Collection. Homeland, 1997.

years of your life by keeping you in hiding. He wins those battles. He wins those days.

How many days has he won so far?

How many more will you allow him to win?

How many days has satan chalked up in the win column simply because you chose not to fight, not to resist?

You have current strength and potential strength to do what God has made you to do. Again, a favorite verse of mine is Ephesians 2:10: "We are his workmanship ... created in Christ Jesus ... for good works ... which God prepared beforehand ... that we should walk in them" (ellipses mine). You are God's workmanship—*poema* or "poem"—you are His writing.

How many days has satan chalked up in the win column simply because you chose not to fight, not to resist?

He has designed you. Only in Christ Jesus will you be able to fulfill what He desires to write about you. He has it in mind and plans to write it. You have to see the work He has prepared for you ahead of time ... and then walk in it or fight through it.

There are the days you don't do the work He has for you. On those days, the enemy racks up one in the win column.

The days satan wins the battle are the days that two things happen:

- **One** – We forsake God and work it out on our own. Jeremiah says, "For my people have committed two evils: they have forsaken me, the fountain of living waters, and hewed out cisterns for themselves, broken cisterns that can hold no water" (Jer. 2:13).
- **Two** – When we choose NOT to follow our great God, we try to use our own strength, which we think will work. We use whatever we can to just get along. Hiding. And what we make is eternally useless.

Is satan afraid when you awake in the morning? Does he say, "Uh oh, they're awake. We better get ready because they're going make this a long day for us"? Or, does satan move the people and traps assigned to you elsewhere because you're no threat to him or his team?

Some people think that they can avoid getting arrows shot at them if they just stand quietly in the back, not making any noise. They think, "I don't want to attract satan's attention so I'll lay low and then whisper if someone asks for the hope within me." They see no hope in someone who is hiding. Yes, that stings. No reason to stir up trouble if you can avoid it.

Sorry, bad concept.

He could not care less where you are; he will shoot arrows at you as much as possible. Plus, he can tell by the look on your face you aren't ready for a battle, so he runs right over you on his way to someone else.

This may seem harsh.

"Steal, kill, and destroy" is pretty harsh!

You think you're avoiding getting hit. But what he sees is weakness and cowardice. You look like a limping antelope to a cheetah. Easy pickin's.

The thing with armor, it's all in the front. It's not built for a retreat and provides no coverage for that. That should tell you something about what's expected of you if you're in the battle. Hiding is not the strategy you think it is. And remember, God's got your back.

By now you are asking yourself, "So, just how do I build the rest of this armor? I've read what it is, who the enemy is, and that I should build it. But how is that done?"

You need a shield because of the arrows. Because of the arrows, you need a shield.

Answer: you need to know what each piece does, and what each piece is based on. We began with the helmet, because without salvation you have no armor to start with. But, we must now know how a shield is built before we learn how to build and grow our own shield.

It is built with some of the same metal: faith/belief. It is the only piece of armor which God states will "extinguish all the flaming arrows" (Eph. 6:16 NIV). Reread that last sentence. It's not that the other parts won't protect you, but God specifically says the "shield of faith." What you actually believe about Him is the only part that extinguishes flaming arrows. And every flaming arrow that is shot at you is a lie.

You could say with a Texas twang, "Them arrer's are errors."

This chapter and the next are inextricably connected. Here's why:

You need a shield because of the arrows. Because of the arrows, you need a shield.

Which came first, the arrow or the shield?

The shield came first.

God has always existed, before time. He existed before He made the angels. As Creator, He has the upper hand. And as Creator, God intends us to know the belief substance and the building of a shield. In the next chapter we discuss the full nature of the arrows.

Truth versus Lie

You must build your shield out of what you believe. That belief must be in truth—the truth of Him.

The first truth you must believe is this: "For God so loved the world, that he gave his only Son, that whoever believes in him should not perish but have eternal life" (John 3:16 NIV). Christ is who He said He is. He was sent from the Father, and we now know He has done exactly what was needed for us to be rescued, saved, and to fight forward for and with Him.

We have the beginnings of that "shield of faith" the minute we become His. The helmet of salvation has some of the same material as what makes the "handle" of the "shield of faith." If you do not get a handle on this, it will be hard to build out the rest of the shield. In Ephesians 2:8–9, God says, "For by grace you have been saved through *faith*. And this is not your own doing; it is the gift of God, not a result of works, so that no one may boast" (emphasis mine).

God gives you the first piece as you get the "helmet of salvation." The faith, the belief, in Him which is your salvation is the substance of the helmet and is also the substance you build the first part of your shield on—Christ is your salvation, nothing else. Christ is your life, nothing else.

But how well do we believe those two statements?

Without this beginning faith from Him, you have no helmet, and no beginning of a shield. Therefore, you have no armor. You are spiritually naked.

You should hear flaming arrows sizzle out on the other side of your shield. If you hear sizzle on your side of the shield, you're on fire.

But when you do believe, you are on to the building process of growing in Him, putting on Christ. Though the enemy lies to you, and he always will, you have a shield which extinguishes those lies. A shield of faith/belief. You want to hear the sizzle of an arrow flaming out? You can. But what causes the arrows to be extinguished? How does faith extinguish them?

You start with, "I believe…" (*pisteuo*: "faith" is the noun version of that word, and "belief" is the verb version). You need a "shield of belief."

We will use "faith" and "belief" interchangeably from now on. Our point is this: put the noun into action. "And without faith it is impossible to please him, for whoever would draw near to God must believe [have faith] that he exists and that he rewards those who seek him" (Heb. 11:6, addition mine). You need that shield of what you deeply believe to hold up against the incoming arrows.

You should hear flaming arrows sizzle out on the other side of your shield. If you hear sizzle on your side of the shield, you're on fire.

I don't remember anywhere in the Bible God saying, "Well, that will teach him a lesson."

He doesn't want you to just know a lesson.

He wants you to know Him, to believe Him as a person.

And then do something with what you believe.

What you know about Him is what is important. There may be a lesson, but just not with the facts only of a lesson. The person involved is God. Lessons are important, but knowing Him well is the substance of your armor. You don't know all there is to know about Christ, and some of what you believe is just untrue. When you believe something about Him which is untrue, and you attribute it to Him as truth, you then build a lie into your shield. Then you wonder why you keep getting struck with flaming arrows right through that spot.

These two facts must be recognized here:

- Not everything you believe about God is true.
- You do not know all there is to know about Him.

Incorrect belief, and incomplete belief. Both are holes in your shield.

Much of what you know is secondhand truth. You heard someone say it, so you believe it only in your mind. So ... your knowledge of Him is somewhat incorrect and lacking. You don't believe it enough to build upon it. Therefore, your shield is incorrect and lacking. You must know what you know about Him, and know why you know it.

Read His Word. Ask Him to show you who He is. I dare you to read the Gospels, and as you read, ask Christ to show you who He truly is. Since He is your armor, how well do you really know Him as armor? His might comes with knowing truly who He is and dismissing the lies you previously believed.

The enemy is shooting at the weak spots and the lies you believe (which he has told you to cover yourself with) and the gaping holes of what you don't know. He knows better than you where the openings and the weak spots are. He has been hitting them for years. All while you've been wondering why you've had such problems in some areas. You have "Hole-y armor," not "Holy Whole Armor."

Believing lies is also like having your armor made of pewter. Pewter is the balsa wood of metals. A shield of worthless metal, lies, will not shield you from the onslaught. The enemy will use whatever he can to get you to build your own armor in the way you may want it—built with lies and misbeliefs.

It is with belief in His might and His character
that you will build your armor.

Some of you are wondering, "If I have His armor, why do I have so many condemning thoughts about myself?" Because what you don't know can cause you harm. It may be because you do not know all His character, the depth of His love, and that He, as your Savior, does not condemn you.

It is with belief in His might and His character that you will build your armor.

Can you, right now, name the dozens of places where God has written about the fact that if you are His, you are not condemned? What about Romans 8:1? Do you really believe those facts to be true truth? How deeply do you know Him and believe Him? All these questions figure in to your shield of faith.

The question is not, "How strong is He?"

The question is, "What is the depth and strength of your belief in His strength and non-condemnation?"

If you can't name it, then do you actually know it about Him?

We are not questioning His strength—we are questioning our belief in His strength. In 1 John 3:19–21, the apostle tells us that we are not condemned because of God's truth:

> *By this we shall know that we are of the truth and reassure our heart before him; for whenever our heart condemns us, God is greater than our heart, and he knows everything. Beloved, if our heart does not condemn us, we have confidence before God.*

But do we believe it?

There is no question that Christ is unquestionably strong. He created everything and maintains everything. We are questioning our own ability to know His strength and the power of His might … and how well we are growing our ability to put on the whole armor of God. The word "whole" or "full" is the Greek word *panoply*. It means the full equipment of the heavily armored foot soldier. We should not go out partially armored. But we do. We must put on the full armor of God and be continually putting it on till we leave this earth.

That lack of deep personal knowledge, is a hole in our shield.

That lack of knowing that He does not condemn us, is a hole in our shield.

All that we don't believe, is cumulatively multiple holes or weak spots in our armor, places where we need to put on Christ. Right now, you might disagree enough to get mad and put this book down, feeling that you have on the whole armor already. The enemy would love to see that happen. He does not want you to increase in Christ's strength.

That is one of satan's big lies. He says that you have all the armor you need. That's just not true. You need a deepening relationship with your Savior and Lord. He IS your armor. We toss around the word "sanctification" and I think we take it too lightly. That's why we have tiny armor. We need to grow up in Him. The offering of Himself perfected it completely for us so that we are now being sanctified—changed. "For by a single offering he has perfected for all time those who are being sanctified" (Heb. 10:14).

As a follower of Christ, you are armed, and need to be more armed today, and more armed tomorrow with who HE is. How you do that is up to you, with the urging of Christ.

When you are trying so diligently to become good, acceptable, and perfect, it is hard to think that you are missing something, or believe an untruth about God. In Romans 12:1–2, God has Paul tell us:

> *I appeal to you therefore, brothers, by the mercies of God, to present your bodies as a living sacrifice, holy and acceptable to God, which is your spiritual worship. Do not be conformed to this world, but be transformed by the renewal of your mind, that by testing you may discern what is the will of God, what is good and acceptable and perfect.*

And, "Trust in the LORD with all your heart, and do not lean on your own understanding" (Prov. 3:5).

Our minds must be renewed as our hearts become trusting.

We are being transformed.

God is changing us.

We are not currently perfect in the eyes of ourselves or of those in this world.

Transformation takes time. It is not done overnight. Just because you are a believer, a Christian, a disciple who wants to follow Christ, does not mean you will be perfect soon. Some days you may grow quickly. Other days you will stall. As you build your armor, the enemy will do what he can to slow the process, to gum up the process, to cause you to build improperly and incorrectly. You know, like building on sand, like not counting the cost before you build.

> **Our minds must be renewed as our hearts become trusting.**

The enemy wants to thwart the process in any way he can. He has had thousands of years of practice at this. So, do not take him lightly. Let the Holy Spirit guide you. "But the Helper, the Holy Spirit, whom the Father will send in my name, he will teach you all things and bring to your remembrance all that I have said to you" (John 14:26). And this Spirit can bring to your mind whatever you have hidden in your heart. "I have stored up your word in my heart, that I might not sin against you" (Psa. 119:11). He can immediately bring to mind what you have stored so you can have it as a portion of your armor. What truth you believe and have stored is valuable beyond your wildest imagination! Stored shield material!

If you don't learn how to build the shield of what you believe, your flesh will continually be stuck by flaming arrows. But every flaming arrow which lands on your shield will be extinguished by the belief you have. Every lie has a corresponding truth.

Have we said enough to convince you to build?

There is hope—the armor is made of Him!

Do you want to be stuck by arrows, or hear them sizzle out as they land and are extinguished on the other side of the shield?

I vote sizzle!

Knowing – Believing – Acting on It

You must know it first, then believe it, then act on it. Mentally knowing and believing are two different things. You can memorize Scripture in your mind without believing it and incorporating it into your heart. The outgrowth of the first two steps is doing something with what you know and what you actually believe.

If you try to change your mind without engaging your heart, it will be easy for the enemy to cause you to choose your wisdom over God's wisdom. "Trust in the LORD with all your heart, and do not lean on your own understanding" (Prov. 3:5).

Again, one very tough thing you must realize is that the enemy knows the Bible better than you. But he does not believe it, because he does not believe God, Jesus, or the Holy Spirit. Neither do his demons. They know about Jesus, but they shudder. They do not know Him as Savior or Lord. The more you know Him, the more you know and believe the Word. So, you are a huge one-up on the enemy.

Before we get into the building of your particular shield, let's look at two examples. We've mentioned Eve and Jesus taking arrows. Let's look closer at the lies.

Eve: shield partially down. Christ: shield up.

Eve Was Lied to and Shot At

She believed the lie—the enemy's false information. She doubted what she said she knew.

Paul brings this up as he wrote to the disciples in Corinth:

> *But I am afraid that as the serpent **deceived** Eve by his **cunning**, your thoughts will be led astray from a sincere and pure devotion to Christ. For if someone comes and proclaims another Jesus than the one we proclaimed, or if you receive a different spirit from the one you received, or if you accept a different gospel from the one you accepted, you put up with it readily enough.*
>
> *(2 CORINTHIANS 11:3–4, EMPHASIS MINE)*

Eve seemed to be misquoting God. We must guess that because what she says does not exactly match what God told Adam. No matter how the extra phrase got into Eve's understanding, satan knew she did not know exactly what

God said. The enemy pounced on the opportunity. He went for a redirect and then the lie. She did not defend herself with her belief in truth, but she believed a lie. This "deceptive cunning," as Paul speaks of it, is classic *gaslighting*. "A form of intimidation or **psychological abuse**, sometimes called **Ambient Abuse** where false information is presented to the victim, making them doubt their own memory, perception and quite often, their sanity."[4]

"Gaslighting" was Merriam-Webster's Word of the Year in 2022.

LIE: (as a question) "Now the serpent was craftier than any other beast of the field that the LORD God had made. He said to the woman, 'Did God actually say, "You shall not eat of any tree in the garden"?'" (Gen. 3:1–2).

PARTIAL BELIEF: "And the woman said to the serpent, 'We may eat of the fruit of the trees in the garden, but God said, "You shall not eat of the fruit of the tree that is in the midst of the garden, *neither shall you touch it*, lest you die.'" But the serpent said to the woman, 'You will not surely die. For God knows that when you eat of it your eyes will be opened, and you will be like God, knowing good and evil'" (Gen. 3:3–5, emphasis mine).

Eve added something which God did not say. But, even with what she got right, she believed what the enemy said over what God said. She chose her own wisdom over God's wisdom.

---

4   https://www.urbandictionary.com/define.php?term=Gaslighting

ACTION: "So when the woman saw that the tree was good for food, and that it was a delight to the eyes, and that the tree was to be desired to make one wise, *she took of its fruit and ate*, and she also gave some to her husband who was with her, and *he ate*" (Gen. 3:6, emphasis mine). And there, we have the fall.

Jesus was lied to and shot at after His forty days in the wilderness.

Jesus defended with what He believed as God's truth. He had a shield, and the arrows sizzled out on the other side of His shield.

LIE: "The devil said to him, 'If you are the Son of God, command this stone to become bread'" (Luke 4:3). A truthful lie. Jesus could have done that.

BELIEF: "And Jesus answered him, 'It is written, "Man shall not live by bread alone"'" (Luke 4:4).

...SIZZLE.

LIE: "And the devil took him up and showed him all the kingdoms of the world in a moment of time, and said to him, 'To you I will give all this authority and their glory, for it has been delivered to me, and I give it to whom I will. If you, then, will worship me, it will all be yours'" (Luke 4:5–7).

A partial truth, and a full lie. satan has some authority, but Christ has all authority. satan has no authority to give Christ.

BELIEF: "And Jesus answered him, 'It is written, "You shall worship the Lord your God, and him only shall you serve""" (Luke 4:8).

satan was given some power: "…following the prince of the power of the air, the spirit that is now at work in the sons of disobedience" (Eph. 2:2).

satan has no authority to give Jesus. Jesus has it all. "And Jesus came and said to them, 'All authority in heaven and on earth has been given to me'" (Matt. 28:18).

…SIZZLE.

LIE: "And he took him to Jerusalem and set him on the pinnacle of the temple and said to him, 'If you are the Son

Jesus defended with what He believed as God's truth. He had a shield, and the arrows sizzled out on the other side of His shield.

of God, throw yourself down from here, for it is written, "He will command his angels concerning you, to guard you," and "On their hands they will bear you up, lest you strike your foot against a stone""" (Luke 4:9–11).

BELIEF: "And Jesus answered him, 'It is said, "You shall not put the Lord your God to the test""" (Luke 4:12).

…SIZZLE.

Do you see how satan slips a lie right in there with our knowledge to see if we will bite?

For each arrow the enemy shoots at you, there is a corresponding truth you can believe in, have faith in, and hold up.

satan came after Jesus, but Jesus didn't stutter. He knew, believed, and could state His belief at the speed of light. So, the enemy had to flee. But don't get all puffed up with pride that you can also see the enemy flee. Remember, "When the devil had ended every temptation, he departed from him until an opportune time" (Luke 4:13).

The enemy may leave for a bit, but he will be back.

Jesus knew exactly what truth He knew, and that He believed it, and He immediately held it up against satan's lies. Can you do that? Neither can I all the time.

For each arrow the enemy shoots at you, there is a corresponding truth you can believe in, have faith in, and hold up.

Chapter 7

Can You Hear the Sizzle?

In all circumstances take up the shield of faith,
with which you can extinguish all the flaming
darts of the evil one.

(EPHESIANS 6:16)

Remember, the shield is the only piece the Bible says will extinguish the flaming arrows. Building a belief shield that extinguishes flaming arrows requires two things:

- Correct placement – building your connected belief.
- Material and strength – belief type and thickness/layering.

How do you build a belief shield? You get better at daily renewing and holding up what you deeply believe about Christ, and, you get better at daily identifying the lies coming at you, then extinguishing them with the belief of Christ. Much easier to say than to do.

Get to know Christ, and you will be ready for the arrows. You could spend your whole life deflecting arrows, and spend little time getting to know the One who you believe, and who will extinguish them. Knowing Him is to build your shield.

Remember, in the Greek language of the New Testament, "faith" and "believe" (noun and verb) are from the same word: *pistis/pisteuo*. Jesus knew exactly what He believed about God and Himself. So, what do you deeply believe about God, Jesus, and the Holy Spirit?

Are you certain about what you believe?

Can you back it up with how He says it?

You can't believe what you don't know. And what you believe wrongly, is actually a hole in your shield.

But don't be deceived! That is incredibly hard to do. Remember, the enemy is subtle, deceiving, shrewd, wickedly cunning … a murdering liar. He will not let you just throw up a few verses at him, and he flees. He will wait for an opportune time, just like he did with Jesus. Again, Luke 4:13 says, "And when the devil had ended every temptation, he departed from him until an opportune time."

Can you identify the lies in your life? And can you block them with corresponding truth you deeply believe in?

Can you identify the lies in your life? And can you block them with corresponding truth you deeply believe in?

Correct Placement – Building Your Connected Belief

Your shield is an imperative piece of armor you must have built well for you to go into battle. But, as you know, you're already in the battle. Your shield must grow, and it must be made of the right stuff, the right substance. Which is faith/belief. So, who do you have faith in? Who do you believe in? What do you actually believe about Christ?

Jesus asked the disciples, "But who do you say that I am? Simon Peter replied, 'You are the Christ, the Son of the living God'" (Matt. 16:15–16). That was the basis for Peter's "belief shield." Though that was a correct theological statement, it was more than just a dry statement of belief. It was about Peter's deep confession about "the person of Christ." It was personal.

Our shields are to be made of what we deeply believe and can state about what we believe about God. Notice how many times we have said "deeply." Tepid belief will just not stand up to flaming arrows. So, what can you state right now? What can you say specifically that you deeply believe about Him? Can you fill up a page with an actual list of truthful facts you deeply believe about who the Trinity is and what They are like? What size is your list?

The size of your belief list is the size of your shield.

How long is your list of what you believe, and can you say it? Right now, stop, and write a list of things you believe about Him.

Is your list short?

———————————

The size of your belief list is

the size of your shield.

———————————

How readily available in your heart and mind are the things that you know and believe deeply about Him? Each truth you actually believe can and should be used as part of your shield.

What you don't know about Him is your part of your unbelief. There is more that you don't know about Him, than you do know about Him. Your unbelief is bigger than your belief. You may have so small a list of what you believe about Him, that the holes in your shield are larger than the pieces that make it up.

But don't give up. Don't stop. Don't just stand there on fire. Build your shield, and then help your brother. God had King David write this about Him: "When the righteous cry for help, the LORD hears and delivers them out of all their troubles. The LORD is near to the brokenhearted and saves the crushed in spirit" (Psa. 34:17–18). David knew what it was like to be wounded, and to wound others. He did not just keep taking arrows; He allowed God to heal his wounds. He believed more and more in God, and he wanted back into battle.

The following is a metaphor, so don't take it too far. Imagine holding a large three-by-three-foot metal shield to protect yourself. Imagine this large shield is made up of one-inch six-sided pieces. Each piece represents a truth you have faith in and you believe in with all your heart. That's 1,296 belief pieces which make up that belief shield. Now, name 1,296 truths you believe with all your heart. Yep. Me too. Tiny shield. The good news is since we are making this up, we don't know how large each piece is or how much it covers. We do know that you have to build up what you deeply believe, and that belief will hold, and shield you.

Your unbelief may be so large that your shield is more holes than shield.

Let's zoom in on a section of your belief shield made from your belief list. These six-sided pieces are connected, with holes where pieces are missing, or incorrect truth is built in.

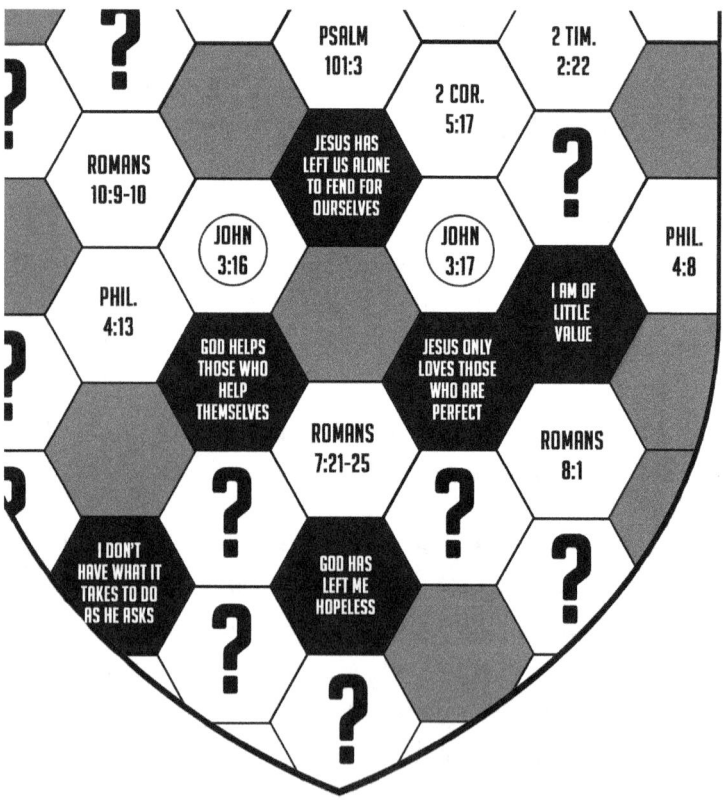

Each piece represents a truth you believe. John 3:16 is your handle. But you have holes where belief is missing.

And you have holes where you believe something which is not true. In the next chapter we'll build pieces of the shield. What truth you do have faith in and believe in will extinguish the flaming arrows. What holes do you have in your shield? Christ has all the truth you can believe in and have faith in. Only you know the holes you have in your shield, and only Christ has the truth for every lie to extinguish the flaming arrows. Start your own drawing of building a shield now. You may think that is hokey, and **Your unbelief may be so large that your shield is more holes than shield.** not necessary. You think you would look foolish ... yet that is another lie. You can only hold up what you have built. You don't want a small holey shield going up against the enemy as we described.

Imagine waking in the morning and there are arrows incoming. Lots of lying thoughts, and "what ifs," and negative things, and tough stuff about your day ahead.... Quick, hold up your shield!! There are holes in it where your belief is missing or incorrect. The enemy sneaks arrows through those holes and you are flaming before your first cup of coffee.

Sound familiar?

The enemy is after you while you sleep and the minute you awake. The shield must be continually built and help you against the lies immediately.

Right about now you are being lied to by the enemy. Some flaming arrows have been incoming. He is telling you it is impossible to know that many truths about our Father, Christ, and the Spirit.

But that's a lie.

It's not the point.

The Trinity and all truth are interconnected and overlapped. Because truth is a Person, and He is available to know. This Person, our Father, and Jesus, and His Spirit, will help you build your shield. Also, you have brothers and sisters in Christ who are standing next to you with their shields. You are not alone. It is not hopeless. But you must start now building your own shield. The great thing about that is this:

The available knowledge of our Father through a deepening relationship is so vast in comparison to the arrows, there is no metaphor to explain it. Truth of Him is infinite!

The available knowledge of our Father through a deepening relationship is so vast in comparison to the arrows, there is no metaphor to explain it. Truth of Him is infinite!

Maybe just start with sticky notes with verses and beliefs on your mirror. Arrange them or line them up. Overlap them like the armor example just shown. Position them so they make sense to you. Cover the gaps in your beliefs. You will be amazed how that visual and your memory can work together and be used by the Spirit.

Mom was right: honesty is the best policy. Sometimes you may believe a lie that you don't want to admit. That alone is a gaping hole in your shield. That's painful, but immediately you must start realizing that what you deny leaves a hole where there needs to be belief in truth about Him.

Shields made completely of Him don't fail.

And thick armor, with thick steel and many layers of material, fails less because it has more of Him. Referring back to the lies we just addressed in the last section, how many verses, or pieces of truth you believe, did we list to combat each lie? Only a couple verses per lie. We could have puts scores of beliefs per lie. But, that's your job. You must build your shield out of what God says is true. The whole Bible is open for you to search

Shields made completely of Him don't fail.

with Him for truth you can believe in. Then, remember what you believe—that's your belief shield.

Christ will not fail, but your belief in Him can. He prayed for Peter that his faith would not fail. Your belief shield will be pummeled regularly at whatever spot the enemy thinks it will fail. Whatever spot your belief is the weakest. Build it!

Let's Look at One Lie

Let's start with one lie the enemy perpetrates on so many people. He will say something like this to you: "You're not really God's child. You're not going to heaven when you die…. This life is all there is…. I mean, look at you."

Now, if you are a follower of Christ and you KNOW that you believe in your heart who Christ is and what He has done for you, and you've said that to Him, He is your Savior! You have placed your faith in Him (see Romans 10:9–10). And because you believe the truth in Ephesians 4:30, you KNOW that you are sealed for the day of redemption by His Holy Spirit, and that when you die, you will go to be with Him. That's fabulous! You are certain of these two things: whose you are, and where you will spend eternity. But, if those are the only two pieces you have on your shield, only two arrows will be extinguished. Many other arrows just fly right past and embed themselves in your soul. Build!

> *You can have Christ as your Savior, and be headed to heaven—but still have tiny armor.*

At times in your walk with Christ, you may tend to only hunker down and hope the battle ends soon. You have little awareness of what's going on around you. As you mature and grow in deep knowledge and belief in Him, you can have more and better armor. And because it covers better and is thicker and more resilient, you can be calmer. Over time we can even gain the ability to see some of the arrows heading our way before they arrive. Even if it only gives us a few seconds to see where the enemy is shooting, we will know after the battle where to repair and thicken the armor even more.

As the battle ensues, we need to remember what Jesus told His disciples:

I'm telling you these things while I'm still living with you. The Friend, the Holy Spirit whom the Father will send at my request, will make everything plain to you. He will remind you of all the things I have told you. I'm leaving you well and whole. That's my parting gift to you. Peace. I don't leave you the way you're used to being left—feeling abandoned, bereft. So don't be upset. Don't be distraught.

(JOHN 14:25–27 MSG)

With Jesus saying He was about to die and leave, I would probably have had no peace, and my heart would be troubled, and I would have some fear! But a mature believer—one who believes a lot, and believes deeply and well—may be able to say to his heart, "Jesus has got this. I will not be troubled. I trust Him and His plan even if it is tough and involves Him going away."

It is possible.

Jesus would not have stated it if it wasn't.

We can have peace.

You need other more mature believers to cover you as you mature. You will also need steps in maturity that describe how we can finally look up from the assault and see what's going on. You will be able to advance during the storm. You need more than a couple of verses for your shield. Keep holding up what you have. He has you! You have Him. Stand firm.

Simon Peter needed to build his shield of belief. Jesus said:

*"Simon, Simon, behold, satan demanded to have you, that he might sift you like wheat, but I have prayed for you that your **faith** may not fail. And when you have turned again, strengthen your brothers." Peter said to him, "Lord, I am ready to go with you both to prison and to death." Jesus said, "I tell you, Peter, the rooster will not crow this day, until you deny three times that you know me."*

(LUKE 22:31–34, EMPHASIS MINE)

When satan asked to test Peter, Jesus did not say no to satan. What Jesus did say to Peter was, "I have prayed that your *faith* may not fail." He prayed that the shield Peter had would hold the enemy back during the sifting. Peter was then tested. He denied that he knew Christ three times. Three arrows landed. Same spot!

> **When you allow arrows to land by saying yes to satan's lies, you end up with less in life, not more.**

Peter verbally denied Christ, but his heart stayed with Him. Then, after he turned back to Christ, he was to go and strengthen his brothers. Peter did this without the Holy Spirit living inside him yet.

We will all go through tough times. Arrows will land.

We may be allowed to be tested by the enemy.

But Christ will pray that our belief/faith will withstand the flaming arrows. And though we may fail three times, it will not knock us down or kill us, but we will turn and follow

Him. When we do, we are to go help others. We know that Jesus prays for us too. He tells us that. "Who is to condemn? Christ Jesus is the one who died—more than that, who was raised—who is at the right hand of God, who indeed is interceding for us" (Rom. 8:34).

satan condemns and demands to test.

But Christ intercedes for us.

Only by your belief/faith in Him and your actions based on that belief/faith will you be able to stand your ground and move forward.

When you allow arrows to land by saying yes to satan's lies, you end up with less in life, not more.

All of the enemy's arrows have lies attached to them. The lies are arrows. The lying arrows are real. The armor is available, but you must build it, grow it, and wear it. Since it is not given to us fully formed, each piece must develop and transform to become more of what it is. Your shield must become more than it is today.

God is with you!

You can do this!

Material and Strength – Belief Type and Thickness Layering

If you want to hear the sizzle, you must have proper placement of correct material. Without the proper materials, you have holes and gaps in your armor. The enemy is looking for those gaps or weak spots … kinks in the armor. Places where your faith may be weak. It is there you need to strengthen the thickness. Truth misapplied makes for thin belief. What arrows keep getting through? Name the lie. Find the truth. Plug the gap.

One example of a material is Kevlar. You're probably familiar with it. It's a heat-resistant and strong synthetic fiber that is found in tires and bullet proof vests because of its strength-to-weight ratio. By this measure it is five times stronger than steel. But, one piece of Kevlar is not Kevlar … it is a piece of fabric. The key is layers laid down one by one that strengthen the entire system. As each layer is added, it adds more strength and adds to its ability to withstand whatever it's defending against. It's strong and also absorbs the energy when it's hit.

This same concept of layering and strengthening is to use similar verses together to build up layers of belief in truth that add strength and the ability to absorb shocks. For example, if you take the topic of condemnation and you reference Romans 8:1, and add to it John 3:17, you get more depth and more strength when they are layered on top of each other.

- "There is therefore now no condemnation for those who are in Christ Jesus" (Rom. 8:1).
- "For God did not send his Son into the world to condemn the world, but to save the world through him" (John 3:17 NIV).

Add John 8:10–11 (NIV) about the woman caught in adultery:

- "Jesus straightened up and asked her, 'Woman, where are they? Has no one condemned you?' 'No one, sir,' she said. 'Then neither do I condemn you,' Jesus declared. 'Go now and leave your life of sin.'"

Now you have three different verses, or layers, that compound the strength to shield you from condemnation.

The armor layers get thick. More impenetrable. Now, how many truth facts do you believe in about condemnation? The shield is getting bigger and thicker.

What you don't know, you haven't built.

Condemnation is one of satan's greatest hits. He wants us to always remember all the things we have ever done. Christ has chosen to forget all of that as He says He separates our sins as far as the East is from the West. It works better if you have belief at your disposal—2 Corinthians 5:17 says:

- "Therefore, if anyone is in Christ, he is a new creation. The old has passed away; behold, the new has come."

There are literally over one hundred more verses if you're willing to look them up and put them in your heart and wear them on your shield. Do an internet search on Bible verses about condemnation. Get a cross reference Bible and add topics that you know are areas of weakness for you such as recurring condemnation. The topics can be endless: guilt, sin, temptation, hate, lusting, grudges, addictions, anxiety, greed, etc. Build your shield.

What you don't know, you haven't built.

If you don't have verses built into your heart, your shield, and the rest of your armor, you are vulnerable to attack on these areas and many more. The enemy doesn't care what topic he uses for an arrow. He only cares that there's an opening to take advantage of. It's up to you to be prepared for the lying arrows on those topics. You know where you are weak and lacking in belief. Start with those you know are your weakest spots and grow from there.

Chapter 8

Build. Build. Build. Build.

In all circumstances take up the shield of faith,
with which you can extinguish all the flaming
darts of the evil one.

(EPHESIANS 6:16)

Let's Build Four More Pieces of Belief for Your Shield

L et's look at what a flame-out sizzle looks like. You will need a lot of parts to be able to be ready for "all circumstances." You must have the corresponding truth for each lie shot at you.

A lie – The enemy says, "You continue to sin, so you are not really His."

But you know God, and He says in Romans 7:15–20:

*For I do not understand my own actions. **For I do not do what I want, but I do the very thing I hate.** Now if I do what I do not want, I agree with the law, that it is good. So now it is no longer I who do it, but sin that dwells within me. For I know that nothing good dwells in me, that is, in my flesh. For I have the desire to do what is right, but not the ability to carry it out. For I do not do the good I want, but the evil I do not want is what*

I keep on doing. Now if I do what I do not want, it is no longer I who do it, but sin that dwells within me. (emphasis mine)

Paul knew this struggle well. But he also knew the One whom he served. Romans 7:21–25 says:

So I find it to be a law that when I want to do right, evil lies close at hand. For I delight in the law of God, in my inner being, but I see in my members another law waging war against the law of my mind and making me captive to the law of sin that dwells in my members. Wretched man that I am! Who will deliver me from this body of death? ***Thanks be to God through Jesus Christ our Lord!*** *So then, I myself serve the law of God with my mind, but with my flesh I serve the law of sin. (emphasis mine)*

Paul struggled against the arrows.

He did not want to give in to their lies.

Do you believe Christ? State it out loud.

Can you hear the sizzle?

A lie – The enemy says, "You don't have what it takes—you will fail!"

But you know God, and He says in Philippians 4:13, "I can do all things ***through him who strengthens me***" (emphasis mine).

First Corinthians 10:13 says, "No temptation has overtaken you that is not common to man. God is faithful, and he will not let you be tempted beyond your ability, but with the temptation *he will also provide the way of escape, that you may be able to endure it"* (emphasis mine).

Christ gives you strength for what He has for you to do, and He will provide a way of escape when the enemy tempts you. Do you believe Him? State it out loud to the enemy.

Can you hear the sizzle?

A lie – The enemy twists truth by saying, "What God *really* meant was...."

But you know God, and He says in John 5:39–40, "You search the Scriptures because you think that in them you have eternal life; and it is *they that bear witness about me*, yet you refuse to come to me that you may have life" (emphasis mine).

John 15:15 says, "But I have called you friends, *for all that I have heard from my Father I have made known to you*" (emphasis mine).

The Scriptures talk about Christ. He is your friend and will make known to you what the Father wants. Do you believe Him? State it out loud.

Can you hear the sizzle?

A lie – Guys, the enemy says, "Look at her. She would be fun, and who would know?" Sexual thoughts abound. Or, something comes up in your Facebook feed … or a YouTube video pops up when you are searching for how to repair something…. Instagram suggests a friend … a girl

126 • *Tiny Armor?*

is jogging … a memory from something you saw years ago … or something you did years ago. Remember the whiteboard and the conference rooms in hell where they plan how to attack you? They use any media, any memory, any situation, and any circumstance.

But you know God, and in Psalm 101:3, David says, "I will not set before my eyes anything that is worthless."

Second Timothy 2:22 says, "So flee youthful passions and pursue righteousness, faith, love, and peace, along with those who call on the Lord from a pure heart."

Philippians 4:8–9 says, "Finally, brothers, whatever is true, whatever is honorable, whatever is just, whatever is pure, whatever is lovely, whatever is commendable, if there is any excellence, if there is anything worthy of praise, think about these things. What you have learned and received and heard and seen in me—*practice these things,* and the God of peace will be with you" (emphasis mine).

Do you believe these enough to practice them?

State them out loud.

Can you hear the sizzle?

> *Your belief is in **Him**, not just the text. Your shield of belief is made of a Person AND what He says. Your shield is built with **Him**.*

There can be other areas that aren't actual lies, but can be wrong thinking which can lead to believing a lie. One area for Mark is when he grew up seeing some people get saved and leave behind lives marked by horrendous things. They had been violent thieves, murderers, rapists, and drug dealers, and the transformation looked so amazing he was struck by the incredible redemptive power in their lives. He thought, what a cool testimony that person has.

Mark accepted Christ at a young age and thankfully never fell into any of those traps. His testimony, while transformative, doesn't seem as dramatic as the stories of people changing a full 180 degrees from where they were and had new lives. Sure, they still had to deal day to day with the ongoing recovery from addictions and time spent in incarceration, but Mark's transformation was no less dramatic from God's perspective. The logic seemed to be, "Surely it took more grace for God to forgive their long list of sins than mine."

> **Your belief is in *Him*, not just the text. Your shield of belief is made of a Person AND what He says. Your shield is built with *Him*.**

Along the way, the Holy Spirit said, "I think you may be underestimating what I did for you. It took the same dose of grace to forgive you that it did to forgive the murderer."

He saw Mark's sin (as He sees all of our sins) as just as bad as theirs. We are not to compare at all. It's a reminder for us not to underestimate what He did for us or take any of it for granted, ever.

You don't just believe truth; you believe HIM!

You don't just believe truth;

you believe HIM!

We need to be shield up to extinguish the flaming arrows of the enemy. We can sense the thud on the other side of the shield.

Can you hear the sizzle of the flaming arrows being extinguished by your belief in the One who saved you?

> **You have to know what you think, believe what you think, and be able to state what you believe to the enemy.... Christ did.**

You may be thinking, "This building armor seems like a lot of work. I could move around better without armor on. I'm more agile. I can dodge the arrows. Right?"

So, how is that working for you now?

Putting Belief into Words

As you sense arrows screaming as they descend on you, and you then feel them pierce your spiritual flesh, you know you have not extinguished them with the shield. The question then becomes, "Can you extinguish flaming arrows without words?"

I don't think you can.

> *You have to know what you think, believe what you think, and be able to state what you believe to the enemy.... Christ did.*

Remember, Jesus did. Eve did not.

We do have the Holy Spirit. We have Jesus who intercedes for us. But that is not an excuse to be lazy and just send up flare prayers when flaming arrows land. When I sense an arrow land, or one coming at me, I state my case in personal pronouns. With my mouth I confess (agree) about what I believe. When you became His, when you *believed*, you believed with your heart that Jesus is Lord. You then confessed (agreed) with your mouth (out loud) that Jesus is Lord. That is what Paul says in Romans 10:9–10. So, if God wants you to say it out loud, He is asking you to say it like you mean it.

Jesus did not stutter when He addressed satan after the forty days in the wilderness. You shouldn't say what you believe as a whisper. You shouldn't say it like you are still unsure. You shouldn't say it jumbled up and forget the main thing you believe. You can't say nothing, and just stand there and let the arrows land. Well, actually you can. But our point here is that you shouldn't. You should verbalize what you believe in a pointed statement to the enemy.

My suggestions:

- Know what you believe.
- Be able to state it clearly.
- Say it out loud.

Now, I don't suggest this in a crowded elevator. But I do believe that you need to state your case, and the truth you believe because of the faith you have in Christ. The enemy is required to flee when you resist.

A good friend of mine, John Harris, who was on staff with me at First Orlando, had the author, Bruce Wilkerson, once tell him, "You need to state a dream [what you believe] out loud to hear it." Saying things out loud makes them more real to our ears, and to those listening. Remember, "So faith *comes* from hearing, and hearing by the word of Christ" (Rom. 10:17, emphasis mine).

Even if you don't remember where it is in the Bible, believe what you believe. Then state it. The One in whom you believe, and the truth you believe about Him, has existed a lot longer than the specific verse and chapter where it is found. Don't let the enemy strike at you for not knowing the address (the verse and chapter). Over time, though, it is good to know where it is in the Bible, because you can go back and read it and show it to others who are experiencing similar flaming arrows.

Make your statements increasingly more personal as though you know God personally and can speak on His behalf boldly. Because you need to know Him more personally daily! We will see Paul ask for prayer at the end of this armor passage.

When the enemy condemns you for something you did, don't just say: *"The Bible says I am not condemned."* And don't just say: *"God says I am not condemned."* The above two statements are not wrong, but it is better to make it personal.

Say something like this: *"satan, my Father does not condemn me; He loves me. And His Son took my condemnation, my shame, and my guilt. My Father said so in John 3:17 and Romans 8:1, if you would like to go look it up. The reason I am not condemned is because I am His. Now, yes, I did that sin, but I am working on not falling into the traps you set. So, you can just go to ... your own hometown."*

You are getting to know God, Jesus, and the Holy Spirit as Persons, not just facts about Them. Use that personal relationship when the enemy shoots. Be a name-dropper! Whatever the arrow is, counter it with what you believe. Then again, if you don't know what you believe, or you believe a lie, you just got lit up. You must get to know our great God and know Him personally and believe what He says is true. Remember, the size of your list is the size of your shield.

Four Ways to Ask God to Help You Build Your Belief Shield

In Psalm 77:1–20, Asaph (the writer, King David's worship leader) records five rhetorical questions in verses 7–9 which he is asking God directly. Whatever Asaph's situation was, it was dire. He was deeply distraught. At times we believe, as it seems he did, too, that God has forgotten us, has no compassion on us, His promises are at an end, and He has no more grace for us. We allow the enemy to get us to question God in so many ways. Yet the answer to all five questions is a resounding, "No." Quite the opposite. Go mark your Bible on this one.

It is amazing how Asaph turns and then speaks to God about how great God has been in the past. Asaph uses the second-person pronouns "you" and "your" for God twenty times. He is directly telling God that He is the One who has done great things and has held things together. Asaph declares to God His mighty deeds, His works, and His wonders from the past. So, rather than believe the lies he believed as truth, the questions in his head, Asaph recalls who God really is and declares that he believes in Him as he says them to Him. Ask God to show you the rhetorical questions bouncing around in your head. Ask Him to remind you what He has done as a loving Father in your own life. He loves it when you love Him in this way.

You can use Psalm 139:23–24 to ask God to search your heart, your mind, and your actions, and lead you in the right direction.

You can take 2 Corinthians 10:5 (NIV), and every day, "take every thought captive" and "make it obedient to Christ." Ask Him to show you how.

You can dwell on James 4:7 and remember that when you resist the devil, he will flee. And then recall that it is the same word as "stand firm" in Ephesians 6:13. In this way, you can build your shield well. Ask Him to show you how to resist.

As you work through assembling all parts of the armor, and growing them in breadth and thickness, you can and should use all the ideas you have just found about building, type of material, and placement, and use all of them for all parts of the armor. You are not going to get by with one verse on righteousness, and peace, truth, and belief.

For the Shield and All the Armor

On the material front a similar concept is chainmail armor. It was in common military use between the third century

BC and the sixteenth century AD in Europe, and longer in Asia and North Africa. It's a series of small, interlocking woven pieces that work together to keep out sharp objects and resist any penetration of projectiles or swords. It takes many small pieces that join together to protect the wearer.

The Romans also used what was called segmented armor. It was made up of metal strips or hoops cast into oval bands and then attached with leather straps for proper fastening. The metal strips had soft iron on the inside and a certain proportion of steel on the outside. What beliefs do you have attached next to each other?

There are different gauges of steel/belief. It can be thicker, and wider, with work on our part through the leading of the Holy Spirit. It's His day job to work with us on developing thicker, stronger armor so we can look more like Christ. You need thick, layered metal. You need to know Him better. You need to double up, triple up, the layers.

Don't Use Homemade Armor

What if I just went out to battle with that Tupperware lid? Homemade shields are made of lies.

> When a strong man, fully armed, guards his own palace, his goods are safe; but when one stronger than he attacks him and overcomes him, he takes away **his armor** in which he trusted and divides his spoil. Whoever is not with me is against me, and whoever does not gather with me scatters.
>
> (LUKE 11:21–23, EMPHASIS MINE)

So, what we put on as armor much of the time is *our* armor, not God's armor. What we hold up against satan is incorrect, incomplete, and has dangerous inconsistencies. It is built of things we think will withstand. Sometimes we have papier-mâché shields. Flaming arrows laugh at it.

What your true shield is to be made of is what you believe about God. How well do you actually know who He is and what He is like? How much of your information about Him is incorrect and incomplete? What you believe must be true, and there must be a lot of that faith to construct a formidable shield. Your shield shouldn't be made of what you want, but of who He is.

When the rest of us advance, your homemade armor is exposed. The author of Hebrews says:

> *You need milk, not solid food, for everyone who lives on milk is unskilled in the word of righteousness, since he is a child. But solid food is for the mature, for those who have their powers of discernment trained by constant practice to distinguish good from evil.*
>
> *(HEBREWS 5:12B–14)*

Can you distinguish well? Truth or lie? What or who do you believe in? The enemy will test this daily.

It may seem at times that you love the arrows/lies more than the One who is to be your armor. You love what the lies may bring you. Flaming arrows have an insidious as well as incendiary part to them. All lies, as with all sin, have a part that seems good and pleasing to the eye, the ear, the mouth, the touch, the mind—all senses. Eve and Adam were only the first to bite the lie.

Remember, the size of your list is the size of your shield. That is also true in the depth and substance you know and deeply believe about who He is. And it is true of every other piece of the armor of God.

- What you believe must be consistently increasing (see Matthew 14:28–33).
- Your belief must be based on true truth completely (see John 8:31–32).
- Build parts of your shield before you need them (see James 4:8; 2 Timothy 2:15).
- A belief in a lie is actually a hole in your shield (see John 8:43–45).
- Sharing shield material is crucial (see Proverbs 27:17; Hebrews 4:12).

Chapter 9

Sharing Shields in Real Time

*...praying at **all times** in the Spirit, with **all prayer
and supplication**. To that end keep alert with **all
perseverance**, making supplication for all the
saints, and also for me, that words may be given
to me in opening my mouth boldly to proclaim the
mystery of the gospel, for which I am an ambassador in chains, that I may declare it boldly, as I
ought to speak.*

(EPHESIANS 6:18–20, EMPHASIS MINE)

Not all people have their shield built to the same
degree or specifications as others. We are all in
process, and the building never stops—because
our belief in God can and should grow until we die. Shields
are always under construction … and under attack.

So, the loving thing to do is to share shields with others individually and also in collective settings. Whatever shield
we have, we can share it, as it is becoming more and more
complete. And we can withstand the test of more and more
arrows.

A young lady in one of Mark's small groups has seen a lot
of tragedy in her life. She is under the pile and the arrows
continue to fly. She is on the ground, unsure about how
to get up. She sent an email to Mark asking for prayer for

several specific areas of her life. It was great to see her reach out while lying on the ground knowing the arrows wouldn't stop and she didn't feel like she could move any more. That email kicked off a larger email from Mark to the entire small group to lift her up in prayer and bring shields over to her to shield her in prayer while she fought to get back up, so her armor would be more effective. All their shields together protected her better than just one shield, especially since her armor felt heavy in the midst of the tragedy in her life.

That's what a small group, or friends in a Sunday school, or a breakfast group, or a group of friends together can do for each other. It's what we are supposed to do for each other. We're in this fight together.

It's good she asked for help.

We wouldn't have known otherwise.

This depth or reaching out about soul issues is vital. Praying for spiritual health and growth is imperative.

> _The closer we are to each other, the more we can share the truth and faith we've found in Christ._

Many people don't have people like this in their lives to call on. They can't share shields. They are face down on the ground with a constant bombardment of arrows from all sides making it harder to get back on their feet to protect themselves. If you think satan will let up on someone who's down, you don't understand how he thinks. When someone is alone and under the pile that is the perfect time to fire arrows. At some point, the enemy hopes they will

---

The closer we are to each other,

the more we can

share the truth and faith

we've found in Christ.

---

give up, discard most of their armor and run off the battlefield never to return. But our armor is built for sharing so that doesn't happen.

Boots on the Ground – Mark's Groups

Mark meets with breakfast groups every morning. Traditional Bible study groups, and also groups of men just eating breakfast together. Men doing life together and studying God's Word, praying for one another, bearing each other's burdens, iron sharpening iron. The effects of the enemy's arrows are discussed a lot. Because of this, these groups of men are close-knit.

Mark remembers a comment made by one of the guys when talking about Jesus. "You need to love Him more than family," the man said. He then said, "I consider you guys my family." That's a great thing to hear from a brother who will show up for a 6:00 a.m. Bible study every week. That level of closeness and transparency leads to a trust that allows each person to open up within the confines of that group and share what's on their heart. They even ask questions that some might consider risky. They meet and share because they have a struggle with some arrow in their lives and are asking for wise counsel from this bonded group. They know whatever is said in the group stays in the group, so no one else will ever hear what he has asked about. I have to think this is what Christ and His disciples looked like: a small, trusted group to do life with, to share burdens and successes and learn from each other. I say more about this in the section below.

On the weekends, it's a group of men, about a dozen guys who have shown up for several years every Saturday morning. Three of these guys grew up in the church and two of them now want nothing to do with church or God or the things of God. Interestingly, one of the three is still okay with church and Christians. But, when he was fourteen in the 1970s, he was told by his pastor, "Well, boy, when you get that haircut, you come on back to church." That young boy is now sixty-two and he still has long hair. He has never forgotten the insult he felt when his pastor said that to him. There was a "personal audio tape" generated that day which remains to this day. Again, he's still okay with church and church people, but he just doesn't go.

What does that tell you?

The pettiness of that comment did not illustrate God's love and caring for the young man. The two other men don't have specific phrases they bring up, but you can tell something similar was said to them. The tapes we mentioned earlier were playing over and over again, causing them to believe that these were not the people they wanted to be around. And to this day, they don't like church or church people.

Not only do we have our own personal tapes, but we might also be creating tapes for others to carry around with them. Sometimes we record things on the tape that shouldn't be there, and we don't understand that our words or looks can last a lifetime. That tape recording may be that one guy's excuse, but it does not give us the okay to help make tapes for people with our insensitive remarks. So, as we meet as followers of Christ, we must share shields, not create bad tapes.

Giving God a Bad Name

Some Christians' words and actions give God a bad name, and satan will use that. Mahatma Gandhi, a spiritual and political leader in India in the early- to mid-twentieth century was a practicing Hindu, and Christianity intrigued him. In his reading of the Gospels, Gandhi was impressed by Jesus whom Christians worshiped and followed. He wanted to know more about this Jesus whom Christians referred to as "the Christ, the Messiah." One Sunday morning Gandhi decided that he would visit one of the Christian churches in Calcutta. Upon seeking entrance to the church sanctuary, he was stopped at the door by the ushers. He was told he was not welcome, nor would he be permitted to attend this particular church as it was for high-caste Indians and whites only. He was neither high caste, nor was he white.

Because of the rejection, Gandhi turned his back on Christianity. With this act, Gandhi rejected the whole Christian faith, never again to consider the claims of Christ. He was turned off by the sin of segregation that was practiced by that church. It was due to this experience that Gandhi later declared, "I'd be a Christian if it were not for the Christians." That's on him. But it's also on us.

Gandhi had tapes playing in his heart and mind, and satan used them to make certain that Gandhi did not come to Christ. You can be responsible for creating tapes for others, even if you don't intend to. At times the Lord will bring memories to my mind. Times when I have offended or misled. As I said, I pray for that person immediately. It's not a time for me to feel condemnation from Him. It's a time to be a part of healing. If possible, I have gone to ask for forgiveness from that person.

This is part of praying for all the saints and a part of armor-building.

When Abnormal Feels Normal

The bad news about trauma in our lives, from whatever source, is that sometimes we have felt that way for so long it feels normal. The enemy can use a slow drift or shift away from the values of Christ. The woman being abused in her marriage may even believe she deserves to be treated that way. She thinks, "My mom and I were always treated that way; it's just how life is. I'm used to it. It feels normal so it's not a problem." The enemy loves to build abnormal into normal so you can't tell the difference. If you can say you don't have any issues or any tapes playing, you're lucky. Or, you're playing the denial tape or the self-righteousness tape so that you feel like you're beyond having any flaws and scars. That in itself is a tape satan wants you to play over and over. You don't have a problem. You're a lucky guy.

> **The enemy thinks, "If we can just adjust the definition of what is right and pure and good, we can sell almost anything."**

*The enemy thinks, "If we can just adjust the defi-
nition of what is right and pure and good, we can
sell almost anything."*

Even the newly renovated Office of Politics is making
great new strides into the society that helps breed a great
deal of shift or division. The enemy wants to make right
now wrong and wrong now right. They also probably have
a church relations department that ensures that church music programs will separate people from each other. No opportunity will be missed by the enemy. We've seen many
failings in this area lately ... and, unfortunately, throughout the history of the church.

Arnie's Story

We both have a good friend named Arnie Weintraub. He
can tell you of the amazing work God will do. For several
weeks in the hospital his wife endured attempts to get a
chemotherapy port put in to allow them to try and jump-
start her kidneys, and perhaps avoid a life of dialysis. Week
after week, the veins would collapse. They would try the
next week, again and again. Then her heartbeat became
very irregular. They finally got one port to work six weeks
into her stay. The doctor said, "We got the scans back and
there is so much scarring in the kidneys from a previously
unknown autoimmune disorder that there is no hope. We
don't need to try the chemo after all. It won't help at this
point."

A couple of weeks into the dialysis, as they got into a
rhythm of learning what dialysis was going to be like, her
numbers moved up. And then moved up again to the point

they stopped the dialysis to see if her kidneys could do it on their own. She got to where her numbers were spot on with no dialysis. They later did a major procedure that fixed her arrhythmia problem.

Arnie emailed me a note with the title: "Miracle?"

Thrilled, I wrote him back that I try as best as I can not to be surprised when I ask the God of the universe for something, and He does it.

I often still wind up surprised.

I try not to be, but I can't always do it. I am reminded that He's God, and I'm not. After she went home, she fell and broke her hip and a few weeks later broke her pelvis. So, back to the hospital. She is now home and doing fine. We're not saying satan did all this to her. But we are fragile, and he takes advantage of all that happens to us while we are here in this fallen world. Yet, as this story illustrates, God can overcome anything satan can throw at us. Isaiah 55:9 says, "As the heavens are higher than the earth, so are my ways higher than your ways and my thoughts than your thoughts."

I knew God had the power to fix this problem and He did. But I was still very amazed with the outcome, even though it's what we had prayed for. It's still surprising to see Him work as only He can. The doctor, as the saying goes, followed the science. The science was clear: there was too much scarring and he had images to prove it. But there is a power beyond, and outside, science that we as finite, created beings simply can't understand, according to Isaiah.

Only through our faith and our prayer can we call on this power. Our lives can be impacted in every realm, including our growth and relationship with Him, through prayer.

The concepts may sound like fiction, but this is real. It happens all around us.

So, get ready. The rest of this book talks more about how to do that.

The Men's Retreat

We share shields collectively, too. We believe the godly spiritual activity described next should take place daily in the real world. The mental assault that comes because of a retreat of this depth, intent, and magnitude is horrendous. But, the enemy was not happy that 120 guys showed up on a weekend men's retreat, that Doug and Mark attended, and that prayer abounded. This is real-world, real-time battle.

Prep for the Retreat

There had been almost a year's worth of prayer over that retreat, which is seen in hell as a really long weekend. This gathering is a great example of sharing armor and prayer.

> ...*praying at **all times** in the Spirit, with **all prayer and supplication**. To that end, keep alert with **all perseverance**, making supplication for all the saints, and also for me, that **words may be given** to me in opening my mouth **boldly to proclaim** the **mystery of the gospel**, for which I am an ambas-*

*sador in chains, that I may **declare it boldly**, as **I ought to speak**.*

(E*PHESIANS* 6:*18–20,* EMPHASIS MINE)

Prayer is one key way the Holy Spirit enables God's power for boldness and in our lives.

We will address this further in the chapter, "Let's Cause a Problem in Hell." The prayer outlined above is a key concept for all of us. The retreat was bathed in prayer months before it happened. I know that because I was part of the team that served that weekend. We prayed for the event, the leadership, the speakers, the participants, the families of the participants—for months. Hundreds of people prayed that way. That's how I know it was bathed in prayer and a shield was prayed over that event. I could all but see that

> **Prayer is one key way the Holy Spirit enables God's power for boldness and in our lives.**

shield as I spent the weekend. I was also on a prayer team that actively prayed for every element during the weekend. We prayed together. We prayed real time, on purpose, before, during, and after each speaker spoke. We prayed all weekend for every event and speaker and participant and volunteer.

I recall one of the things that stood out at my first retreat. It's the rows of 8.5 x 11 sheets of paper that lined the two sides and the back of the entire chapel. It was the name and thirty-minute time slots of everyone who was praying real-time for the event—twenty-four hours, for three days— while the event was going on. That is in addition to all the other prayers. I like an organization that recognizes the need for intentional prayer. James 5:16b (NIV) says, "The prayer of a righteous person is powerful and effective." I can tell you it is. But it requires strenuous intentionality. The group that prayed for that event did it every day.

When Nehemiah was leading the effort to rebuild the walls of Jerusalem, he prayed for six months for that project and it only took fifty-two days to finish. That ratio is probably about right. Our intentional prayer for our families, friends, relatives, coworkers, and yes, political leaders—all of them—and praying for ourselves is vital to our growth. We can't grow without it.

None of satan's henchmen gets the weekend off when this event happens. The dates are circled on many whiteboards in hell. They see a pattern emerging. Everyone assigned is required to be there because this could get out of control. If 120 guys leave a retreat on fire (not from arrows) and they talk to another 120 people in their churches, and at work, and in their neighborhood … this relational gospel stuff can quickly spiral out of control. It's like a rock thrown into a pond. Once the ripples start outward, it's unstoppable. The enemy hates that! The number of arrows assigned to each participant of the event is of course part of our metaphor. But you bet it was more arrows and more troops than would normally be assigned. And satan probably assigns more to the leaders, and still more to the speakers.

You get the idea. This is a really bad weekend from satan's perspective. They have three phases to impact this.

Pre-Retreat

satan wants to make sure the attendees get cold feet. Make sure their kids say, "Dad, do you really have to spend three full days away from us?" His wife may ask the same question. He may wonder how uncomfortable it might be getting with a bunch of other guys he doesn't don't know. He starts to question his decision. But he needs this respite. Some guys may think of backing out because they worry that time with other guys talking about topics might call them out or embarrass them. Because, after all, they may not feel like a strong Christian and assume the others will have their life totally together, and either been to seminary or the equivalent and they can barely remember John 3:16 and a couple of other verses. They will be found out to be a "less mature" Christian and that too could feel embarrassing.

What if penetrating questions are asked and you're not comfortable being that open, especially with guys you don't know? What if it's just a self-help group that will feel like a waste of time? And you'll get behind at work. And oh, by the way, there is already strain on your marriage. Things just aren't going well between you; being away when she's a little annoyed will just make it worse.

Maybe you should just not go.

Ever been there?

Arrows!

During the Retreat

What if some of those things you were worried about came true, even a little? You carry with you the thoughts of your marriage. You may assume everyone else's marriage is wonderful and yours is the only one that's not. That's embarrassing just to think about. Or feel you have to admit it. Then you're sleeping in a dorm setting with a bunch of other guys. They're snoring. You're losing sleep. You wake up tired. It's hard to concentrate.

satan doesn't care how he distracts you. Fatigue, thinking about things at home that may be going well or not, or that big meeting you can't work on because you can't even have your phone for three straight days. Who does that? This is the twenty-first century. I'm pretty sure there's a constitutional right to not separate you from your phone against your will. It's right after Separation of Church and State: Separation of Phone and Owner.

Arrows!

What happens at the retreat is not what was feared. In fact, the guys were accepting, and the worship was great. It was a safe spot away from the normal distractions. And a volunteer leader at the event set the expectation that we would pray to the God of the universe about any issues we had as a group. Even if we needed to pray for them for ten minutes we would. One person at his table was able to garner the courage to say his wife had gathered all her things the week before and left him shocked and shattered. This actually happened in Mark's group. The guy said he was beside himself and had a gun on the table when his mom walked in. The situation was embarrassing enough but for his mom to see that he was considering suicide, it was well beyond embarrassing. All of it crushed him.

The group got around this guy, put their hands on his shoulders, and prayed for him. It made a huge difference to know God was there and working in the real world with real world problems that we normally don't talk about, especially with people we don't know. Shortly after that another person found the courage to follow that example and said he had been having some major doubts about his walk with God. The process was repeated. And then repeated four more times on different issues over the next day. The walls were now down. They could voice any issue in their lives and the guys wouldn't judge them. In fact, they supported each other with the power of God which they knew transforms lives. But they had forgotten about it because of the despair and rote activities of life.

Arrows!

Post-Retreat

As good as this experience was, it led to the final phase of satan's attack—post-retreat. All weekend all the minions of hell were assembled outside this room at the camp. They understood they were losing the battle and if they didn't make an impact now it would be a whole lot harder once these guys dispersed all over North Texas and Oklahoma. More weekends on alert only to lose. They showed up with tons of arrows and extra fuel to light them. They were prepared as they descended on the event.

Except for one thing.

They didn't realize how much prayer had been poured on this entire event over the last year.

A solid year of prayers for protection for all 120 guys individually. They soon found that the arrows just bounced off whatever was around this building. That didn't stop them though. They just kept firing until satan himself stepped up and said, "Save your arrows. This isn't going to work. We'll have to just focus on post-retreat." It was indeed a bad weekend for satan and his troops.

They understood they had lost and they were not happy about it. Their thoughts were now about nothing but Monday morning and their revenge. Oh sure, they could do a few things here and there: one guy will forget his keys and one will have a flat tire on the way home. As Monday morning dawned, the guys who foolishly failed to take Monday off (as suggested) to sleep later and recover a little, quickly rushed to the office or to log on to their laptops at home to make up for all that lost time. They were tired and behind and that's a pretty good setup for the enemy. Someone being a little off their game. A perfect time to remind them that while enjoyable, that weekend was not who they really are. They are actually the same people that showed up on Thursday with all the pieces of their lives either under stress or broken.

satan will hit everyone after a mountaintop experience.

Sure, they got to talk about it and pray about it and that felt nice. But now is the time for the enemy to reinforce that this is their real life, not that one-off mountaintop experience. They may have really enjoyed worshiping together with a bunch of other men. It may have tasted like a little slice of heaven on earth and maybe they were able to set down their load for seventy-two hours, but then reality sets in. That was fun, but it's over. The enemy wants to make sure they know the whole ride is over and it's time to get back to reality, the arrows. It's not how you came to the weekend; it's not who you are.

Of course, that's all a lie but in his thirst for revenge and more, for his embarrassment, satan unleashes every weapon at his disposal. That shield of prayer for each guy is gone unless they prayed it for themselves that day. Unless they put on the armor piece by piece, they would need to see the lies for what they are: life-altering, soul-sucking defeat that comes from believing the lie of someone who wants their ruin.

satan will hit everyone after a mountaintop experience.

The leaders, the speakers, the guys who volunteered their weekend to serve others—they will all come under attack. No one is exempt. satan wants revenge on all of them. But the quality of the armor of each man will determine their reaction to the attack. So those guys have a choice. Some will believe the lies of the enemy because by now it's a comfortable burden. They're used to it, so putting that on instead of the armor is what's natural. Some know to expect it. As with the event, they and others will pray in depth for protection. They know that Matthew 16:18 is true. That the gates of hell will not prevail against them.

They're not running scared. They're aware of the battle and prepared. They have prayed in anticipation; they have girded themselves with the whole armor of God. They know who the Victor is for these upcoming battles. And it's not satan. As mad and frustrated as satan may be, they know he can't win unless they let him. And they have no intention of letting that happen.

Some of the guys who were at the table got everyone's phone numbers and created a text string of these newfound friends who would share a shield with them. They knew enough to know there is no reason to walk onto a battle-field by yourself any time.

So, don't do it. You may have had an experience like that before. But knowing what's coming is called situational awareness. It's anticipating what's coming because you understand your enemy and have taken the appropriate action to counter it. Weekends like these are for collectively building and reinforcing armor and sharing shields.

When Your Heroes Leave to Be with Jesus

During a read-through of this book, I lost my dad. I actually hate that phrase. We didn't lose him. We know exactly where he is. He's with Jesus.

Dad had a rough fight with some bad skin cancer. They had to remove a five-by-four-inch section of his scalp and skull to attempt to get it all. He also had a bad infection. In the middle of all this, I remember that Paul says in 2 Corinthians 5:8 that he would rather be absent from the body and to be at home with the Lord. That is true for me. I believe it to be true with all my heart. Dad did, too. He knew Christ well. But I am tearing up even now. I do miss him greatly.

He held his shield up for me in my life. He lifted me up in prayer so, so much. He was a dedicated man. I have the lunch pail he used in the sixties sitting on a bookshelf where I can see it from my writing chair. He was a faithful man who provided for his family. I remember as a kid running to meet his truck when he got home. The rule was the first kid to run to the car got to carry dad's lunch pail into the house. I selfishly don't think I let my sisters win very often. As an only son, it was a joy to see my dad come home each day.

Next to the lunch pail on the bookshelf is a ChapStick. It is the one I used to put some on his lips, when he could not lift his arms the day before he died. He was so very tired. It is the last thing I got to do for him before I said, "Goodbye, I'll see you tomorrow."

Overnight his lungs became so inflamed with the infection that he and the meds could just not fight it off. His whole body was shutting down. They had to intubate him, which is something he really did not want. But he was so weak and suffocating that I assume he allowed it. He did not want heroics. When mom and I arrived early that morning, as he lay there, they said he could hear us but could not move. Mom was holding one hand; I was holding the other. It was time to let him go. As I held his hand, he squeezed it tightly twice. I know in my heart that was a signal: "I love you. Now, let me go home!" I will ask him when I see him. In Psalm 116:15, God says, "Precious in the sight of the LORD is the death of his saints."

It did not feel precious to us in that moment.

It felt like a flaming arrow, as if the enemy was saying, "God is not good! He took your dad!"

But that moment was precious to Dad, and to the Lord, because he was going home. The enemy wants to use the death of my dad to take joy from us as family and friends. He wants to use it as an arrow. He wants us to ask, "Did we do all we could?" "Did we ask enough questions?" He wants us to ask those things so he can lie to us, saying, "If you had just done more, Jim would still be here." He wants to tell us that we failed Dad. But we will not let him. We will not believe the lies of arrows.

We do believe Dad is home with Jesus. Death is not natural. It is not how God intended things. But He allows all of us to choose during our lives to believe, or not believe, that He exists. And that He is a good God even in the midst of death. Remember, He says He is with us as we walk through the valley of the shadow of death. It is our choice to stay in the valley or allow Him to walk us through it. Our choice. Read that again—our choice. I say that because with our choice, we can choose to respond or not to respond to Him. But along with the ability to choose Him is the ability for others to choose badly, and for the enemy to run somewhat free until his time comes to an end. That day seems closer every day.

Death, where is your sting? I can tell you where. The sting was in that hospital room, but only for a time! First Corinthians 15:54–57 says:

When the perishable puts on the imperishable, and the mortal puts on immortality, then shall come to pass the saying that is written: "Death is swallowed up in victory." "O death, where is your victory? O death, where is your sting?" The sting of death is sin, and the power of sin is the law. But thanks be to God, who gives us the victory through our Lord Jesus Christ.

I and my family believe this.

Though there may be a sting for the season, the arrow intended to push us back, to kill us, to steal our joy, does not work. It sizzles out on the other side of our shields. Why? Because we hold onto these truths. We believe them. They are part of our belief shield, and that shield of belief extinguishes the flaming arrows. There are many tears. But not tears of loss. They are tears of great memories and a future where we see Dad again, with our Lord!

Chapter 10

Leading under Fire

*...praying at **all times** in the Spirit, with **all prayer and supplication**. To that end keep alert with **all perseverance**, making supplication for all the saints, and also for me, that **words may be given** to me in opening my mouth **boldly to proclaim** the **mystery of the gospel**, for which I am an ambassador in chains, that I may **declare it boldly**, as **I ought to speak.***

(EPHESIANS 6:18–20, EMPHASIS MINE)

What does this look like for those in leadership of an event like the retreat just mentioned? This, and all the work of the church, is what satan hates to see. He will do whatever he can to make the process of putting any "armor-sharing" event together more difficult. He will try to convince the volunteers they're too busy to give up parts of five weekends. They do, after all, care about their kids' development. And if you coach your child's sports team, surely taking care of your family is more important than taking a few weekends and three long days just for some strangers you'll never see again. The leader of the next men's event remarked to me about how satan tried to put obstacles and distractions in his way and the life of his family. Remember, if he can't get you to buckle under the pressure, he will use those around you to impact you negatively.

His story goes like this:

> This weekend retreat is designed to do many things, but the two biggest, in my opinion, are to help men deal with the junk in their past and to train up Christian leaders. That said, we are hugely successful in creating men who are engaged for Christ, and more often than not, go back to their home churches and become lay leaders. Not just pew-warmers on Sunday. It's an enormous blessing to see these guys engage in their faith, their marriage, and their church.

> God can overcome anything satan can throw at you.

> That said, after serving for several years I was asked to be the rector (the guy in charge on the upcoming weekend). They ask the potential rector a year ahead of time if he would be willing to serve in that capacity.

> Knowing previous rectors, I heard often that it is a huge blessing, but it doesn't come without a cost. They had all told me that the year of preparation also included a year of increased spiritual warfare. I have a wife and three teenage children. So, when I considered this great blessing for me against the idea that the evil one and his imps would come after me and my family, I was concerned. With that as the pivot point in my decision-making process, I told the board of directors, "No, thank you."

Fast forward a year and a half and the board asked again for me to be rector. After lots of prayer and council with my wife and close brothers in Christ, I agreed. I picked amazing younger men to surround me on the leadership team and set off to do those things I knew how to do with a passion.

One week during our leadership meeting, I asked the men to reach out to their section heads and see if anyone had any prayer requests. A few days later I asked if any prayer requests had come in yet. On a team of 120 there had to be someone needing prayer. I was shocked when the grand total of requests came to two. Either the leadership did not filter down the requests, or the men didn't respond to a group text … or the men had all said they were "fine." So, I thought I would use the title of rector and text each guy individually that night and ask if there was anything I could pray about for them. Within an hour, forty had responded. I was blown away.

By the next morning I had another sixty. I had no words to describe it. One hundred men had asked us to pray for things that were intensely personal. Later that day, one of the board members called me to see how things were going. I paused, trying to find the right word to answer him. He offered up, "It's a grind, right?" I said, "No, as of last night, it has turned into something different." It profoundly changed my outlook on things. So, we prayed as a leadership group, many through tears, for over an hour at our following leadership meeting.

I individually asked the men again a few weeks later and was blown away again. Out of 120,106 replied. This time I asked if my brothers would pray for me. I had been struggling for a long time to find two new employees for my business but more importantly the evil one was attacking my wife through her work. So, here was the ugly beast that I fretted over a year and a half earlier. I was so blessed with men texting me that they were still praying for Shannon a month later. This whole prayer thing has blown me away. And while things are still crazy with my wife's work, and I have found only one of the two people I need for my business, I am realizing it's not about getting what I wanted, but has been to my benefit. It is about the transformation of the peace He gives us as we go through these things.

I have thought and prayed that God would help me understand why we went from two responses to one hundred in one day. I think it's because the original was sent out in a group text format. But once someone asked them personally, they were willing to share. Which points back to the theme of the weekend, "Relationships." Men hunger for close relationships, but our culture tells us we have to be strong; we have to man up. And while yes, some of that is very necessary, there are times when it's okay to admit you don't know what to do, that you don't know where to turn to. I think a good first step in finding a few men to be willing to stand side by side with you in life is an honest request for prayer. I know it has transformed me.

This concept doesn't just apply to men's retreats. If you're involved in a mission trip, a board or committee at your church, you lead a small group, or teach a small group, you should expect to encounter resistance from the enemy. If you're working for the good of the kingdom, you will see increased attacks. But just in case you say to yourself, "Well then, I'll just keep my mouth shut and not stir anything up by serving. I'll just sit here quietly. I won't be a target," you misunderstand how this all works. The enemy doesn't just shoot at people in the fray; he will shoot at you because you're a Christian and not his. You can't just hide in the corner to avoid the arrows. By now you know that arrows are a metaphor for whatever the enemy uses to divert your attention away from God. You can't hide. You weren't built to hide. If you are hiding, then satan wins anyway because you're on the sideline instead of in the game, and he'll take that tradeoff any day.

The Trinity Shares

When you think of Jesus's last prayer for His disciples, and for us, you can't escape what He said in John 17. He only had one other remaining prayer while on earth, in the Garden of Gethsemane, so this was one of His most significant prayers. And it was for us! That we would be protected, not taken out of the world, but protected from the evil one while in the world … and that we would be one—that we would share in the life of one another. He knew what we were in for after He left and so He gave us the Spirit.

In John 17:9–23 (NIV), Jesus says:

> *I pray for them. I am not praying for the world,
> but for those you have given me, for they are
> yours. All I have is yours, and all you have is
> mine. And glory has come to me through them. I
> will remain in the world no longer, but they are
> still in the world, and I am coming to you. Holy
> Father, protect them by the power of your name,
> the name you gave me, so **that they may be one as
> we are one**. While I was with them, I protected
> them and kept them safe by that name you gave
> me. None has been lost except the one doomed to
> destruction so that Scripture would be fulfilled.
> I am coming to you now, but I say these things
> while I am still in the world, so that they may have
> the full measure of my joy within them. I have
> given them your word and the world has hated
> them, for they are not of the world any more than
> I am of the world. My prayer is not that you take
> them out of the world but that you protect them
> from the evil one. They are not of the world, even
> as I am not of it. Sanctify them by the truth; your
> word is truth. As you sent me into the world, I
> have sent them into the world. For them I sanc-
> tify myself, that they too may be truly sanctified.
> My prayer is not for them alone. I pray also for
> those who will believe in me through their mes-
> sage, that all of them may be one, Father, just as
> you are in me, and I am in you. May they also be
> in us so that the world may believe that you have
> sent me. I have given them the glory that you gave
> me, **that they may be one as we are one**—I in
> them and you in me—so that they may be brought
> to complete unity. Then the world will know that*

you sent me and have loved them even as you have loved me. (emphasis mine)

His belief in you covers you. And your belief in Him can help cover the souls of the person next to you and vice versa. You all can become one. The turtle, or Tortuga maneuver, used in the movie *300*, has been used by many armies. It involves all of them being covered by the collective sharing of shields, so everyone is covered. Like a turtle is. It works because the group trusts each other and shares a defensive movement as they move forward. We often miss what comes with being a disciple of Christ in the West because we are trained to be self-made.

Fiercely independent. An army of one. What? That's the dumbest slogan ever.

There is no such thing as an army of one, by definition. Look up the definition of "army" and it means a collection of people working together. You are not an army of one; there's no such thing. You're not on the battlefield alone, or at least, you shouldn't be. We don't need an army of one; we need an army which IS one, as God is One. Together.

Fiercely independent. An army of one. What? That's the dumbest slogan ever.

Jesus prayed for you and me and all the saints in that prayer. The disciples heard it first, but it echoes throughout history to include us. This prayer is His heart for us just as much as the disciples in front of Him. In verse 11, He asked that the Father would protect us by the power of His name. So, if you think you're in this fight alone, remember this verse. Make it part of your belief shield. He even references the loss of satan from the kingdom when he fell. He hasn't forgotten what happened to satan.

He is aware of what the enemy is doing. In case you think He might be occupied with other things and might miss what satan is trying on you, rest assured He has not lost track of everything satan does, and He has promised to protect you. It's not based on your ability to protect yourself…. He is the armor.

He prays that we would thrive in whatever situations we might face. And that can mean ugly situations: that illness you despair over, the job or relationship problems you face, the family issues that seem intractable, or that divorce that just won't let you see yourself as anything but a failure. The enemy would have you believe that these situations disqualify you from the fight. But they do not. That is not how God sees you and He doesn't want you to see yourself that way. The truth He knows is the truth you need to know and believe. That truth will build your shield; it will reinforce belief areas that are weak. Romans 8:37 says, "No, in all these things we are more than conquerors through him who loved us." But you must believe it.

Jesus saw you and your situation down through history when He said this prayer in John 17. He meant it to be as applicable today as it was when His disciples listened in on that divine conversation between the Father and the Son about them, and about us. Yes, Jesus was praying for His disciples at a time they were distressed to hear they wouldn't see Him anymore. But it was also to you and me and the situations we face today. He prays for areas in which we are distressed, or worn thin. That shield of belief must be built.

We are not an army of one. Christ's desire is that we be one as He and God and the Holy Spirit are One. They are there for each other, forever!

Friendly Fire

When we are not one, we often get hit with lies that are fired at us from those around us. Yes, satan uses others to fire shots at us. Fellow Christians who miss the mark as we walk with them, and it leads to disillusionment and hurt. I don't understand why they call it "friendly fire." It's anything but friendly. It's only called that because it is from those who are supposed to be on our side, and by our side. The arrows in this case may not be shot directly at us, but are shot at our behaviors or statements, seen by fellow believers, which may cause them to question everything about their own faith. They get defensive, then they start shooting indiscriminately and hit us.

Our building of armor and moving forward threatens those near us who say they want that, but really do not. Sometimes though, the arrows may be shot directly at us from "enemies in the camp." Infiltrators. Betrayal. Christ understands that. But that is for another chapter.

Should we really be counting only on others around us to guide our faith, our belief? Yes and no. Yes, we need others to share a shield. But no, we don't need others perpetrating non-truths and misbeliefs about Christ, or about us. It's hard to not grow disillusioned when we're in a setting that is advertised as Christian, but the behaviors observed are in contradiction to that. One of our close friends, who is a very strong believer and has been at the forefront of various ministries, recently sent us a letter describing the long-term effects of just that kind of behavior.

It's painful to read. A couple of quotes from the letter were: "We've [he and his wife] lost complete faith in the Big 'C' church. We've lost trust in the theologians who were instrumental in shaping our faith. We've abandoned several authors who speak about the truth of biblical principles but fail to demonstrate those principles in the way they live their lives." He also referenced the downfall of a mega-church and the pain that still causes. The most compelling quote was perhaps the last one: "My helmet is on and I'm holding onto a broken shield with all my might."

What great transparency to share this with us. Does that sound like a cry for help?

This is a solid soldier with a long track record of managing large ministries who has observed things that have hurt him and his wife. And it has them in search of what he calls, "Another church that will not burn us again."

He is on the battlefield. He is in need of others around him to share their shields with him as he gets off the battlefield to heal, for as long as that takes.

> *"My helmet is on, but I'm holding onto a broken shield with all my might."*

"My helmet is on, but I'm holding onto a broken shield with all my might."

From his experience, Mark guesses that about seventy percent of the hurts of those in the church are from this kind
of friendly fire. This is from years of being a part of church
leadership. They're not arrows fired from outside but rather are observed on the inside of the church. Make notice
who you are co-laboring with. Be aware that your life is
having an impact on all those around you.

It's much like the caught-and-taught concept of parent-
ing. Your kids pick up everything you say. Not just the
well-prepared statements you want them to remember.
They notice how you address your spouse when you're
tired or irritated. We would love for those things not to be
written down in their memories, but they are. Don't be a
perpetrator of friendly fire. How you live your life matters
to everyone around you. It's not just you and God on this
journey. Be mindful of how you treat others. Especially
those in the foxhole with you. It matters.

It matters to your Sunday school teacher. If you feel that
that you just "have to" meet them at the end of the class to
show them how they were wrong, you might be doing that
just to win an argument and to show them and yourself just
how smart you think you are. Unless it's blatant heresy,
invite them to coffee or lunch and talk about it. You may be
ignoring the fact that they work just like you do. They have
kids, and lawns to mow, just like you. And they missed
most of Saturday's football game, that you saw, because
they were studying to share with you what God's Word
had to say. You are not providing feedback to your music
minister when you just have to point out how few, or how

many, hymns they either did or didn't sing and how disappointed you are about it.

Get a grip. How about thanking them for the time they take for you? Encourage them. There are plenty of other people and things to discourage them. Don't be one of them.

Mark loves to watch wildlife shows. The one thing you quickly learn is that the predator only wants to achieve one thing. Break one animal out of the herd and then they can capture it, if they're big enough. Nothing worse than watching a cheetah try to take down a water buffalo. It's not going to happen. But if they pick the right-sized prey and are fast enough to keep up and can get one to bolt away from the herd in the panic of the moment, they have a great chance of bringing home dinner. If the herd sticks together and no one bolts, they are all safe.

satan does the same thing. The enemy wants you isolated from your herd. If you aren't in a church family, a Sunday school class, or a small group that knows almost everything about you, or praying with your spouse, you're isolated and in danger—whether you know it or not.

Armor protection also comes in the form of being with other soldiers, together, side by side, in unison. Overlapping shields. So, the environment where you wear your armor is important, too. A single soldier on the battlefield, even with armor on, is more vulnerable that an army moving forward with intention. Armor on and overlapping to cover the gaps. That's where the protection comes from.

Life is a team sport.

We're not meant to do this alone.

Make sure that doesn't happen.

You control the situations you put yourself in. So, be aware of the impact of those decisions concerning the people who you are with. Do they have shields? Any armor?

Because sometimes the arrows come from within the camp.

Chapter 11

Flaming Arrows – What They're Made Of

*In all circumstances take up the shield of faith,
with which you can extinguish all the flaming
darts [arrows] of the evil one.*

(EPHESIANS 6:16; "ARROWS" FROM NASB)

Flaming arrows—they are arrows, they are flaming, and they are pointed at you. This is what your belief shield is for. I don't know why the *English Standard Version* translators decided to use the word "darts" instead of "arrows." It seems to diminish the ferocity of the attack. I choose to use the word "arrows" from the *New American Standard Bible* translation. No matter, they are flaming. And every arrow has a lie. They are from the liar. They are all based on his research about you and all that is on that whiteboard in hell. It is personal. We can't say this enough … he wants to do anything he can to take you out or push you back, and cripple your ability to function for God in any form or fashion. And don't think these arrows may come only one at a time, or are small and extinguishable by yourself. Yes, some of them may be small and insidious, so they land without you even knowing.

But it is not like swatting at little gnats.

All arrows are live ammo.

Sometimes it's an aerial onslaught like the opening scene in *Gladiator* when Russell Crowe's character, Maximus, says, "At my signal, unleash hell."[5] And yet, the enemy is at times so subtle as to use small, barely *lit darts* to take you out or knock you back. Think of the old movies with aboriginal men using blowguns and darts with poison tips … and those darts are on fire.

Any and every visual your mind conjures up, he will fling at you in as vicious a way as he can. You must know the sin which entangles you so easily and know how Christ can stop it. If we are to have any success at all, we have to know the types of arrows used, and the way the enemy uses negative and positive arrows. We must know the lies of the arrows, and even how the enemy can use an arrow twice. Whether in waves, or small and subtle, all arrows are blatant lies.

All the media, all the recordings, all the tapes, all that planning in hell for what can be put before your eyes, in your thoughts, and anything that can remind you of past or future failings, are all designed to destroy. If this thief can't kill, steal, or destroy … he will redirect, distract, create detours, divert, confuse, disturb, amuse, and entertain you. He will nag you, scold you, light you up, and attempt to reprimand you even though he has no authority to do so. He is allowed to try, but he cannot actually reprimand you. He is not your father. But he will cause you to think

5   Scott, Ridley, dir. 2000. Gladiator. DreamWorks Distribution, California. 155 minutes.

your Father is saying it. But it's satan faking a reprimand. He will cause wandering, drifting thoughts of worthlessness. He will cause you to think more of yourself than you should. He will cause prideful thoughts, and make you think, "I got this," launching out on your own, doomed to failure because you didn't talk to your true Father about it. You were listening to satan's lies. He will cause you to jump off financial cliffs of your own making. He will push you to think you are "all that," and cause you to demand from relationships, rather than asking how you can give to your relationships. He will attack anything that looks like God, has the aroma of God, or is facing in God's direction.

Arrows Can Be Almost Anything

He will twist any and all of the good things that God made and create arrows out of them. The enemy has blinded the minds of those who do not believe Christ.

Paul wrote, "And even if our gospel is veiled, it is veiled to those who are perishing. In their case the god of this world [satan] has blinded the minds of the unbelievers, to keep them from seeing the light of the gospel of the glory of Christ, who is the image of God" (2 Cor. 4:3–4, addition mine).

Are you as exhausted after reading that paragraph as I was after writing it? The enemy is all that, and more. This chapter and chapter three and four are frustrating to me. It's so easy to focus on the enemy too much and worry about arrows instead of focusing on Christ and building His armor with Him. But it is absolutely imperative that we know who and what is against us. We are confronting formidable spiritual rulers, authorities, cosmic powers, and spiritual forces, so we need to know how they design these flaming arrows to shoot ... at you.

> *The enemy would have you think that he has the upper hand.* ***He does not.***

Do we really know the enemy and his attacks on us well enough to understand his arrows? Do we know Christ well enough to be ready for whatever the enemy shoots at us? Do you know yourself well enough to know where you are weak? For at that place, Christ can be made strong through building His armor there.

If you are not building your shield by now, stop reading, and begin that process. Get a notebook and start drawing six-sided pieces and name them with truths you believe. We don't want you thinking of arrows without immediately asking the Spirit to show you some truth you can deeply believe to build a shield with. Work on your shield as you finish the book—because flaming lies are flying at you right now.

The enemy would have you think that he has the upper hand. *He does not.*

Just because Christ will help you build your armor for whatever the enemy is planning does not mean you just sit there and expect Christ to do all the building. You work together with Christ on your armor. Never forget John 10:10b: Jesus came that you could have life and have it abundantly. It sure does not feel like it sometimes. Those who don't know Christ are currently perishing. They are the ones still under capture. They are blinded; there's no abundant living there. Yet Christ has come to rescue them, and He wants to use you to do that. We'll discuss this work in length in the last chapter.

So, how do we, on the pointy side of the arrows, define what lying flaming arrows are? Are we recognizing arrows? "Re-cog-nizing" means remembering. It's the cognitive action of your heart and mind remembering what whacked you and why. When you find yourself at odds with God and His ways, something flaming has landed and pushed you sideways. If north is your focus, anything that pushes you any degree south is an arrow. Since we realized from chapter one that Christ is our focus, then anything that takes our focus off Him is an arrow. This is hard to grasp. But if Christ is my life, then anything not of Christ is a false life. We know from building a shield that we must consistently know Jesus more and more and use the belief we have to hold up against the lying arrows. Therefore, an arrow is anything which is contrary to the truth of God and His ways. Anything.

Every lie is an arrow, and every arrow carries a lie.

Knowing what is contrary to God's ways, no matter how subtle or vicious, depends on us knowing what is true. We can't compare truth with a lie if we don't know the truth. Recognizing arrows—distinguishing lies from truth—requires seeing that they are contrary to truth, even as they are approaching. We never said this would be easy. I be-

————————

Every lie is an arrow,

and every arrow carries a lie.

————————

lieve the hardest thing on this fallen planet is knowing Him well enough to know when something is not of Him.

As a follower of Christ, the more you can recognize the arrows and extinguish them, the more you can become fit soldiers with the spiritual armor of Christ. And you can move forward for the sake of others who are currently choosing to believe the lies. But, one small deviation after another, and you will find yourself even facing away from Christ, much less following Him. The arrows will always nudge us away from truly following Christ. *When you believe a lie, or disregard the truth, your shield gets weaker, not stronger, against the arrows.* And more lying arrows will follow.

For reasons I don't fully know nor comprehend, God allows choice to play out. One of my professors in seminary made a statement about choice I will never forget. He said, "If you were to ask a girl to marry you, and she could not choose to say no, would her yes have any meaning?" That still haunts me. God allows me to choose. He allows you to choose. And He allows our choices to affect each other. This will not last forever. When Christ returns, He will put things in order. And choice will end for satan and his minions. We will know the whole Trinity as They truly are. But for now, we do not see clearly and many times choose unwise ways. We can choose to know Him and follow Him, or we can choose not to. And to choose not to follow Him is to choose the arrows: "Whoever is not with me is against me, and whoever does not gather with me scatters" (Matt. 12:30).

Have we said enough for you to realize that you are in a war zone? You must choose Christ. You must choose His armor. The great news is that Jesus is building your shield with you to protect you and extinguish these arrows. He knows what being shot at is like.

The First Arrows on Earth

What must it have been like to be the recipient of the first arrows? Eve and then Adam were the first two to get lit up by the enemy. After the attempted coup in heaven, satan and one third of the angels were cast out of heaven by God. They became demons, and their leader became satan the devil. They then decided they were going to try to take out God's highest creation, man and woman. And now, specifically, anyone who looks like Christ. In most instances, he is not just after you, but everyone you are with and everyone you care

I hate to say it, but many days our minds are weary. We forget what we know. We forget our armor and have misplaced our shields like our car keys. We are naked souls, open targets for the enemy to easily strike.

for. He knew just how to get Eve and Adam. And he knew he would get the whole human race. Collateral damage counts on his whiteboard. But now, when you "take up the shield of faith to extinguish all the flaming arrows of the evil one" (Eph. 6:16 NASB), you are doing it not just for you, but for others as well—collateral success.

Who in their right mind would just allow those arrows to pierce their spiritual flesh day after day?

We would.

We do.

Because we are not in our right minds.

We are in *our* mind, not the mind of Christ. Even though as believers we have the mind of Christ, at times we choose to use our old minds instead. The enemy pummels our spiritual flesh and material flesh with these arrows, these lies, day in and day out. He is relentless. And when we believe these lies, our shield is either tiny or down.

I talked about these lies earlier—three personal lies the enemy shoots at me regularly:

- A lie – The enemy says, "God still condemns you for your past."
- A lie – The enemy says, "You don't have what it takes."
- A lie – The enemy twists truth by saying, "What God really meant was…."

The enemy personalizes all arrows. Your whiteboard lists your weak spots. When the devil went after Christ after forty days in the wilderness, he went after Him personally in ways he has no need to go after us. The devil knew Jesus, who He was and is. The devil knows who you are and what will work on you.

But those moments when we are thinking with the mind of Christ and not believing the lies, we believe the truths He knows are true, and we are able to push forward, extinguishing arrows before they affect us. We hear the sizzle on the other side of the shield. "'For who has understood the mind of the Lord so as to instruct him?' But we have the mind of Christ" (1 Cor. 2:16). We must know the truth He knows.

> *I hate to say it, but many days our minds are weary. We forget what we know. We forget our armor and have misplaced our shields like our car keys. We are naked souls, open targets for the enemy to easily strike.*

Our mind of Christ, our memory of what truth we believe, is important in ways which we can't even imagine. And the enemy has plans which undermine our thoughts and shoot past our tiny armor.

The Enemy Has Two Parts to His Overall Plan

Part A – The enemy does not want any of us to become followers of Christ.

Part B – If we do, he wants us to be retreating, rather than advancing, most of our days.

He fires the arrows at us to distract us, to diminish any effect we have in the kingdom so that he can steal, kill, and destroy anything of God in our lives. He wants to stop us from even thinking about following Christ and affecting others in any positive way. He will use anything that works.

Remember, satan and his demons constantly adjust what is on the whiteboard. The arrows can be small, which causes them to be almost undetectable. Like being off just a little on a measurement, direction, or setting on a rifle. A little off in a small distance is magnified over long distances. The enemy will stop at nothing until God stops him. He will distract, redirect, or paralyze, and use any method he can to keep you from moving forward in Christ and making any difference in His kingdom. Nothing is off limits. There are no rules. No chance to say, "I forgot my armor. Can we have a do-over?"

As hard as it is to believe, the enemy was your father at birth. Ephesians 2:1 says we "were dead in the trespasses and sins." And John 8:44a tells us, "You are of your father the devil." Not just the Pharisees. All of us. And we all need to be adopted into God's family. We need to become His children and to be grafted into His eternal family: "And I will be a father to you, and you shall be sons and daughters to me, says the Lord Almighty" (2 Cor. 6:18). Once we do, we not only get sealed for the day of redemption, but we also get that suit of armor to begin to defend ourselves and to grow in who He is. Remember, all parts of the armor are of Him and from Him.

The arrows are not rubber, suction-cup tipped arrows. Those toys from our childhood are the farthest from what he shoots, and what he intends. These are designed to destroy anything of God's purpose in our lives, anything that resembles our Father, anything that has the love of Christ attached to it.

Learning to live abundantly in the midst of flaming arrows—that is our lot in earthly life until we step over into eternal life.

Since your armor, shield, and sword are to be used against satan's flaming arrows and to help others who have been hit, the shield must withstand all types and sizes of flaming arrows. You can deny and hide, or you can put on the whole armor of God and move forward. He has you.

For some, those who do not know Christ, the words of John 8:42–47 (NIV) are haunting:

Jesus said to them, "If God were your Father, you would love me, for I have come here from God. I have not come on my own; God sent me. Why is my language not clear to you? Because you are unable to hear what I say. You belong to your father, the devil, and you want to carry out your father's desires. He was a murderer from the beginning, not holding to the truth, for there is no truth in him. When he lies, he speaks his native language, for he is a liar and the father of lies. Yet because I tell the truth, you do not believe me! Can any of you prove me guilty of sin? If I am telling the truth, why don't you believe me? Whoever belongs to God hears what God says. The reason you do not hear is that you do not belong to God."

Part A is still true in their lives.

All Arrows Have Lies

Many days—not all, but many—I wake and the enemy is attacking my thoughts and trying hard to get me depressed or off topic immediately. He hits me with condemning arrows. I know in my heart and my mind that I belong to Christ and am being used by God for the sake of others. But still the arrows fly. The condemnation begins as soon as my eyes open, sometimes even before.

I know that my thoughts must immediately be about God upon awakening. My first conscious thought should be that God is my sustainer. But in my mind, I sometimes go with the lies the enemy is telling me. And instead of hearing the sizzle of a flaming arrow going out on the other side of my shield, I am getting burned the minute the alarm goes off. Before I even realize it, I am fighting thoughts with *my* strength instead of taking them captive and making them flame out because of the truth I believe about Him.

Learning to live abundantly in the midst of flaming arrows—that is our lot in earthly life until we step over into eternal life.

I have to be reminded that in Ephesians 6:10, God says, "Finally, be strong in the Lord and in the strength of his might." It is in His strength I rely. And His strength is derived from putting on His armor. I sometimes also try to reason *my* way through things instead of simply believing that God has this and that He has me. I know that faith in Him who has saved me and will give me strength must be the first truth I believe in the morning. What does it mean to rely on the strength of His might? I have to reread chapter one often. Instead of worrying and trying to do life on our own, we give it to Him:

> *Don't fret or worry. Instead of worrying, pray.*
> *Let petitions and praises shape your worries*
> *into prayers, letting God know your concerns.*
> *Before you know it, a sense of God's wholeness,*
> *everything coming together for good, will come*
> *and settle you down. It's wonderful what happens*
> *when Christ displaces worry at the center of your*
> *life.*
>
> (PHILIPPIANS 4:6–7 MSG)

If I do not remind myself that prayer should take the place of worry, or allow the Spirit to remind me that I am His, and He's got this, then I am not taking "every thought captive *[and putting the flaming arrows out]* to obey Christ" (2 Cor. 10:5, addition mine). Taking every thought captive means I know the lies well enough to see the thoughts they intend. I can see the arrows coming, and I place my faith up against them. It is true that it is His armor, but I must be reminded to put it on and hold it up. I am not on my own since the armor of God is His armor—including the shield—and is made up of who He is. Every piece of the armor is Christ. The armor of God is like Iron Man's armor but much, much better because it's soul-deep internal and external armor. Or the armor of God is like *The Matrix*, where you can pick arrows, like picking bullets, out of the air before they hit. You can see the flaming arrows coming. You are thinking right now, "No, I can't. They just come out of nowhere." That is the way it seems.

———————————

As we increase in the knowledge of Him, we'll know how to discern lies from truth.

———————————

However, over time you grow and come to know Christ well enough, and believe Him deeply enough, that your shield is ready and able no matter what arrows fly. But that doesn't mean satan won't up his game. When he does, we up our game.

As we increase in the knowledge of Him, we'll know how to discern lies from truth.

*His divine power has granted to us all things that pertain to life and godliness, through the **knowledge** of him who called us to his own glory and excellence, by which he has granted to us his precious and very great promises, so that through them you may become partakers of the divine nature, having escaped from the corruption that is in the world because of sinful desire.*

(2 PETER 1:3–4, EMPHASIS MINE)

Do you know Him well, and do you do what He says here? It will keep you from the lies and desires the enemy shoots at you.

The enemy will lie to you positively, too. He will tell you that "you've got this," or that "you are good enough to get this done." He will attempt to land arrows of pride and self-reliance that will cause you to forget to rely on God. He will attack areas where you think you are strong.

If you take pride in an area you don't think you need to worry about, guess what door you open?

Pride.

If you're proud of your humility in a certain area, you have just made it an area of vulnerability. How often do you have a short prayer time in the morning and then run off to tackle the day, only to realize about two hours in you are failing even though God is right there? He reminds you of His presence, and you have to say to Him, "I'm so sorry I forgot You were here and that I forgot to ask You about all I had planned today." Oh, how often I have done that. My self-sufficiency and commitment to me overshadowed my talking and walking with Him. Those days I seem to realize that some arrows disguise their flames in shiny, glittering compliments to myself.

A Woman's Perspective

A female friend of ours gave us her thoughts on arrows that sometimes hit her.

She gave me this list. While not specific to women, they seem to be common themes in women's temptations. Lying arrows concerning:

- Jealousy
- Anger
- Sex
- Money
- Food
- Pride
- Dissatisfaction
- Comparison

Then she thought about it some more and said that from her experience, the two biggest that she had seen were comparison and jealousy. The following are her words on the subject.

> Never before in history has there been a force dictating human cultural norms and values like the current influence of the mass media. Up until the last two decades or so, the main influential entities on cultural norms and values were parents and the church. The prevalence of the internet, cellphones, and social media have now usurped the influence of both parents and the church on the formation of personal paradigms and values.
>
> The influence of the mass media is especially problematic for young women for whom the culture has been particularly difficult to navigate. Unrealistic expectations of physical beauty placed on women, for example, have been problematic for women for decades, but the upsurge in mass media usage has created an entirely new set of challenges and issues for women in particular. Two of those issues that create struggle and temptation for Christian women in particular are comparison and jealousy.
>
> Theodore Roosevelt once said, "Comparison is the thief of joy." Whether married or single, Christian women can easily fall into the temptation trap of comparing themselves to the other women they are exposed to in the greater society, but also to the women in their spiritual circles as well, who are most like-

ly being influenced by the same mass media sources. Without the proper filter for these issues, Christian women can find themselves in a state of joylessness in their lives and questioning who and what stole that joy.

Comparison can creep up on women insidiously. It starts out pretty innocently; maybe it's seeing those perfect party cake decorations for your five-year-old's birthday party on another woman's Pinterest board and wishing YOU could be that creative. Maybe it's seeing that woman's "Day in the Life" video on YouTube where everything goes exactly according to her plan for the day. Meanwhile, you feel like if you can get the kids out of bed and out the door with all their clothes on for school, without losing your sanity, that you're lucky, and that NOTHING seems to go according to plan for your day. Maybe it's seeing her Instagram post where she's on an exotic vacation with her handsome husband and they seem to be having the time of their lives, not having a care in the world.

Comparison has taken deep roots in our culture, to the point where most women do not even see it anymore. We have allowed comparison to be almost a default mindset because we are not satisfied with the mission that God has given each one of us in this life. We want what SHE has instead of being grateful for what God has given us for the purpose He has for our own life. We are basically dissatisfied with who God made US uniquely to be.

One of the problems with comparison is that the natural next step is jealousy. Jealousy is an even more critical issue because not only does jealousy indicate that you want something someone else has, but it takes it a step further. Jealousy is a sign that not only do you want what the other person has, but also that you do not want that person to even have it! You feel resentment that they have it! That is very dangerous ground to be standing on.

The Bible has a few things to say about the issues of comparison and jealousy: "Not that we dare to classify or compare ourselves with some of those who are commending themselves. But when they measure themselves by one another and compare themselves with one another, they are without understanding" (2 Cor. 10:12). And, "A tranquil heart gives life to the flesh, but envy makes the bones rot" (Prov. 14:30).

These are two perfect truths from God you can place on your shield of belief to extinguish the arrows of comparison and jealousy. But you must believe them.

Chapter 12

Flaming Arrows –
How They're Used

*In all circumstances take up the shield of faith,
with which you can extinguish all the flaming
darts [arrows] of the evil one.*

(EPHESIANS 6:16, "ARROWS" FROM NASB)

There are many types and sizes of arrows. The enemy will use any flaming thing he can throw at you. The opening scene of *Gladiator* has the Roman army using catapults to hurl oil-filled, flaming balls that burst against the trees, raining down liquid flames. They use huge numbers of flaming arrows. And not just one at a time. Thousands at a time. There are days it feels this way. The enemy can be relentless. I have noticed sometimes, but not always, that when I am moving forward or I am closer to "the goal for the prize of the upward call of God in Christ Jesus" (Phil. 3:14), the enemy will either distract me or shoot all that he can at the moment at me.

Christ grabbed hold of me for a reason. He loves me, and He has work for me to do. If Ephesians 2:10 is true, and it is, Christ has work for you to do in the kingdom. Work made to fit you perfectly. Not just your employment, even though that is a ministry God has given you, but all works Christ has for you. The closer I am to His work, it seems the greater the volume and more specific the arrows which fly.

Some arrows are tiny. As teens, we'd play a nutty game where two of us would sit a few feet opposite with a small pile of wooden matches. One of us would place one match tip down on the concrete (outside!) with one finger on the top like you would hold a football waiting for the kicker. Then we would flick it with our other finger, causing it to light on the concrete as we sent it flaming end-over-end toward our opponent and his pile. I'm not recommending this as a game; just saying we played it. The intent of the game play was to light your opponent or keep him distracted while lighting his pile.

The enemy will use catapults, flaming arrows, and even flicked matches to try to take you out. Anything he thinks he can land, he will try. He does not know your thoughts, but he knows your reactions. He has been paying attention and knows what lies, what condemnations, what distractions, get you off track, or knock you back, or cause you to be so fearful that you go cower in the corner. He does all this with the intent of harming you in any way he can. He is not playing a game: he is playing for keeps.

The Enemy Uses Arrows Twice

The enemy will remind you of past sin. It may have been years ago! How can that still have an impact? A sexual encounter from a decade, or decades, ago can be used by the enemy to remind you of sinful, physical joy. By allowing him to draw you into that thought, he is using an arrow a second time.

The enemy will remind you of every time you were bullied, picked last, neglected, abused, tormented, or just disregarded and made to feel worthless. The enemy can bring those lies back to mind immediately and tell you they are true, just like he lied to you back then.

How do past events hold such sway over us today? Jesus paid the penalty for our sins on the cross. When satan tries to remind you of past sins, envision Christ holding a receipt for that sin. In fact, why not paste it on the outside of your armor like a bumper sticker: "Paid in full." Do you believe that? Put it on your shield. When the enemy has wrapped an invoice around an arrow, and he says, "You should pay for it," hold up the receipt on your shield and remind him that it's paid in full!

How do we pray for the past when the enemy wants to use an arrow twice? When I was praying years ago, asking God how to fight against the arrows of reminders of past sin, He gave me this: "Pray for them." Then it hit me what He was saying. I can pray for whomever God puts on my mind. I can also pray for whomever satan puts on my mind. So, when the enemy brings up past sins, and anyone comes to mind along with that sin, I start praying for that person immediately. I sense satan's frustration. That was *not* his intended effect. I have noticed over the years that he flees immediately. He surely does not want to cause more prayer to happen.

He knows he is going to burn forever, so he is going to do anything he can now to burn up what he can. And if he can hit you in the same unguarded spot, why not? And there are times he will wait and come back later. The arrow worked the first time. satan says to himself, "Why not just remind him of the wound? Kick him when he's down." Only God

A match can burn twice.

knows what He allows him to do. And thankfully, God does control even this strategy, so that these attacks can be for our growth and good. Imagine how much worse it could be if the enemy were released completely for a time. I pray I am not on earth when Revelation 20:3 is fulfilled no matter how you interpret that verse.

When I was a kid, I saw a trick one of the guys in our neighborhood played on an unsuspecting friend. He asked, "Hey, you want to watch this match burn twice?" Of course he did. That can't happen! Well, it can. The guy with the match lit it, then blew it out and quickly pressed it on to the other guy's forearm. The trick only worked once! We didn't need a reminder that this could happen at any time to anyone once a match was lit. We should be that leery of satan.

A match can burn twice.

The enemy will hit the same spot twice, or three times, or a hundred if he thinks he is getting through. The enemy may say, "You are condemned because of what you just thought!" You say to him, "I am not!" You quote the verse that you are not condemned. The enemy then says,

"Yes, but you do the same thing all the time." He will say that there is an end to God's non-condemnation. You then might tend to agree, and say, "Yeah, you're probably right. If I keep struggling with this, I probably am condemned." At that point, the enemy just shot an arrow right through a thin spot on your belief shield because you *did not deeply believe it.* You just had just a passing inclination toward it, and quoted Scripture without conviction. You need layer upon layer of what you believe in, what you have faith in, *who* you have faith in. Just because you can quote Scripture doesn't mean you deeply believe it.

It's not just me, is it?

I sometimes find myself singing songs during worship and my mind has wandered off.

I'm saying the words, but don't mean them because my mind is elsewhere.

I repeat to myself truths from Scripture that I actually believe.

But do I believe it, or are they just words?

If I sit still long enough and talk to God about it, He will show me where my unbelief is and where my under-belief is, and you'll have another one of those "you of little faith" moments.

The apostle John wrote how the Holy Spirit helps in this area: "But the Helper, the Holy Spirit, whom the Father will send in my name, he will teach you all things, and *bring to your remembrance* all that I have said to you" (John 14:26, emphasis mine). You need to give the Spirit some spiritual metal to work with on your shield. Focus!

Can You Actually Identify the Lies in Your Life?

We are going to hit this again here—you must be able to identify the lies and make the substance of your shield the truths you believe. When you begin this process, you'll start to hear the sizzle of arrows flaming out on your shield. Remember, you should hear the sizzle on the *other* side of the shield, because if you hear sizzle on your side, you're on fire. If you don't learn to identify satan's lies, and you don't build every part of your armor, you may be left with your salvation helmet, but you are mostly spiritually naked, and mostly wearing arrows. And, you're on fire. You look like a lit porcupine.

One other element we can miss is what comes from having the Holy Spirit reside within us. Remember the charge to Moses to take his sandals off because he was on holy ground? Think of this. Wherever you and I go is holy ground. You have the Holy Spirit in you (Moses did not), and the Spirit's presence makes wherever you're standing holy ground because of who He is. You may think that but you're not holy enough for that to be true. You're right, but He is holy, and He does make it true.

We are not perfect on this side of heaven.

How does God see you if you have accepted His gift of forgiveness?

For every lying arrow, there is a corresponding truth that you can believe. Do you?

Perfect!

When He sees you, He sees Christ.

Because of that and the Holy Spirit in your life at all times, you are seen as holy by God. But the Holy Spirit also still sees the imperfections in our lives and helps us want to fix them. He convicts our hearts of sin and enables us to want to change sinful behavior if we will lean in. When that lying temptation arrow comes, and it will, you can take that thought captive or run with it and see where it takes you.

> *For every lying arrow, there is a corresponding truth that you can believe. Do you?*

You may let a lie grow slowly over time into something much larger than you would have ever allowed originally if you had known where it was going to lead. Notice you have control of how this turns out. But, how do you know that it is getting out of control? If you notice yourself saying something like, "It's not that big a deal," or "It's not going to hurt anyone," or "No one will even know I entertained that thought longer than I should have," you're deceived into thinking it's a small arrow. A firefly. Instead, these thoughts should strike you as a *red flag*. Ignoring red flags makes all other flags start looking much paler. The bright red flag can become a soothing blue that is hardly noticed.

Over time you can be standing in a field of red flags and not see them around you. The Holy Spirit will be waving His arms about them, but if you ignore Him, you can easily wind up in a field of flags and not notice it until the burn gets really bad, like a long day at the beach without sunblock. The burn comes now, but it is felt later.

satan can't take your salvation. All he can do is try to get you to make yourself ineffective. If you're distracted, for example, with work, or political divisions in the nation, or even good things like being on too many boards and committees at church, you will be ineffective. He will use worldly and spiritual battles. He might even succeed in getting you to do something that would discredit your reputation and, by association, God's reputation because people know you are a follower of Christ. So, when that affair is made public, life collapses around you. That's a double win for satan when that happens. But you won't fall alone. Every member of your family is now involved. Your friends and even extended family members will find out about it. Your relationships with your closest family members may be shattered. God loves you and you are saved, but the consequences of your actions do not go away simply because you are saved. Even non-Christians know this is true. It's been said, you can ignore reality, but you can't ignore the consequences of ignoring reality. And that's true.

No one wakes up one day intending to find themselves standing in the middle of field of red flags not knowing how they got there. They didn't even see the first red flag. It is often a long, slow journey to get to this point with some denials about what's going on and the impact of what's happening. Again, the Holy Spirit will make you miserable about your sin. It's His day job. You actually want Him to point your sins out to you. He wants to

help you avoid them right off the bat by capturing every
thought and dealing with them quickly, extinguishing their
potential impacts. That's the easy way. Or you can do it the
hard way, having to undo the mess you've wandered into,
hopefully with as little damage as possible. What little red
flags come to mind right now?

Rebuilding Is Reminding and Reinforcing Soft Spots

Once an arrow has landed and sizzled out, it will leave a
mark, whether in your flesh or on the shield. We must remind ourselves of who Christ is in the area of our lives the
enemy is attacking. I had to do that this morning. One arrow which the enemy regularly shoots at me is, "You will
never get it right." I could write another whole book about
where that came from, but suffice it to say, satan regularly
shoots that lie at me. The older I get, the more I hear them
sizzle on the shield. And yet, he still lands some. And they
stop me dead in my tracks. Not dead … just motionless.
Not mortally wounded … just stunned for a minute.

Years ago, I would have been wounded by, "You will never get it right!" I am not saying I won't again. The enemy
may up his game. But over the years I have put layer upon
layer of deeply believed truth about who Christ is and who
He therefore is to me. You see, you can't just place truth on
your shield where an arrow almost got through. That will
hold for a moment, but the enemy will test it by shooting at
it. You can't just place it there as truth. You have to deeply
believe it. That is a personal act. You must believe with all

your heart that Christ is who He says He is. And with every sizzling arrow, He proves it.

The enemy is looking for soft spots in the armor.

He will try an old soft spot in the armor from time to time because he used to land an arrow there. This particular morning, I was working on finishing a final content read-through on another book, *Fish Prison*. I am not an editor. I overlook typos. I sometimes make mistakes in grammar. I forget to make certain that there are segues from one topic to another. I miss a lot! So, as I'm reading through it one more time, the enemy says, "You're not going to get this right. You are going to miss something, and you will be embarrassed." For one moment he had me. I sensed that incoming arrow flaming and screaming toward me.

The enemy is looking for soft spots in the armor.

Then the Holy Spirit brought to my mind that Christ loves me and He has this. He has called me to this. And I can do the things He has asked me to do with His strength. Other people will come along to help me do what I am not good at. So, I pause and say that to the enemy out loud. I hear the sizzle, then I have a good, deep sigh. I smile, I inhale, and I keep reading.

Christ is the one who can take words and make them make sense to someone. I will try my best with His help, then allow God to use these words to help someone know Him better. Remember John 14:26: "But the Helper, the Holy Spirit, whom the Father will send in my name, he will teach you all things, and bring to your remembrance all that I have said to you." So, let the Spirit do in your life one of the things He does so well—reminding you who Christ is, and what He says to you. It is great building material.

Chapter 13

Spirit Sword

...and the sword of the Spirit, which is the word of God.

(EPHESIANS 6:17)

Y our Spirit sword *is* the Word of God. It is made up of the words of God. It is designed for you to move forward as well as help define all other parts of the armor. Without His Word, the other pieces of the armor cannot exist in your life. As you move forward in life, as Christ asks, you will approach the gates of hell. You will need this sword. Nearing the gates of hell is not an option. Since we live in enemy territory, we either accidently come near the gates, or approach them on purpose as we rescue others. Either way, we are ambassadors here. We live for the kingdom and speak for the kingdom. Our armor is not just to defend or hunker down. More about the gates of hell later.

As you move forward, there are times you will need to stop and shield up before you move further. This preparation will depend on your sword—your main offensive weapon.

Do not let satan be the only one in the fight with an offensive arsenal.

You have access to the largest and most formidable spiritual arsenal rescue team in all of eternity, the Trinity! All three persons: our Father, His Son, Jesus, and the Holy Spirit all want to give you what it takes

Do not let satan be the only one in the fight with an offensive arsenal.

to stand firm, move forward, and rescue others. And when you use who They are, the enemy is required to back off. But do you? Everything They stand for, everything They said, and everything They are, is a weapon of mass recovery for you and for others.

This sword is the Word. The Word is Christ. It is Him you are proclaiming, and Him you are thrusting forward as you go about life proclaiming the gospel.

> *In the beginning was the **Word**, and the **Word** was with God, and the **Word** was God. He was in the beginning with God…. And the **Word** became flesh and dwelt among us, and we have seen his glory, glory as of the only Son from the Father, full of grace and truth.*
> (JOHN 1:1–2, 14, EMPHASIS MINE)

Christ Himself is what you carry in front of you as the sword. So, we are wearing Christ as the armor, we have the Spirit living in us, and we have the Word of God as we lean into life.

The Spirit will use the Word to help you cut through obstacles and enemies in front of you. Again, "the Helper, the Holy Spirit, whom the Father will send in my name, he will teach you all things and bring to your remembrance

———————————

Moving further into enemy

territory is not optional.

Tomorrow is coming.

———————————

208 • *Tiny Armor?*

all that I have said to you" (John 14:26). The Spirit will guide this sword so you have what you need. You will know what to say.

> *And when they bring you before the synagogues and the rulers and the authorities, do not be anxious about how you should defend yourself or what you should say, for the Holy Spirit will teach you in that very hour what you ought to say.*
> (LUKE 12:11–12)

Most of us are not going before authorities, but we might. We surely are going before our friends, our neighbors, and those we work with. Jesus promises that the Spirit will guide our words. Remember when satan was tempting Jesus? Remember what Jesus said to him? "But he answered, 'It is written, "Man shall not live by bread alone, but by every word that comes from the mouth of God"'" (Matt. 4:4). The Word of God, what God said, is more important than anything else you know. Christ is the living Word and yet quoted the written Word. I know this is confusing, but we only need to know that knowing who God is, and what He has said, is what the Spirit will use as you move forward, not only to defend yourself but to set other captives free, just as Jesus did. All three Persons of the Trinity are involved here.

> *Moving further into enemy territory is not optional. Tomorrow is coming.*

"So do not worry about tomorrow; for tomorrow will worry about itself. Each day has enough trouble of its own" (Matt. 6:34 NASB). But I do worry about tomorrow, and today, and sometimes about repeating the past. But if we have armor, and it is Him, and we have the Spirit sword, we can not only move forward in life, but we can be more than conquerors. We can be rescuers.

This spiritual sword is designed to cut through the entanglements of your life and the lives of others, to unentangle yourself and them from sin and the world. Because His Word is true, Christ and His Word will help you discern your thoughts and intentions. You have the potential to bring truth to every conversation and person you meet. But do you? Do you have the sword ready to help others see the truth of Him in a situation, or is your sword in the sheath? And what does that look like? I can tell you that keeping your sword in its sheath is a bad idea. I had an actual physical sword and left it in its sheath. Apparently, some moisture got into it, and it was rusted pretty bad. If you don't often use your sword, you will not know its condition.

"For the *word* of God is living and active, sharper than any two-edged sword, piercing to the division of soul and of spirit, of joints and of marrow, and discerning the thoughts and intentions of the heart" (Heb. 4:12, emphasis mine). Let that sink in. Do you want to know the intentions of your heart? God will use Scripture to expose your intentions. You want your heart better daily so that you can help others daily. And this Word that you wield will last forever: "The grass withers, the flower fades, but the *word* of our God will stand forever" (Isa. 40:8, emphasis mine).

If you want to know yourself and your heart, which is what God really cares about, Scripture is the method He uses to expose to us our heart's condition. This passage says the Word of God is active. Have you ever found yourself reading a passage you've read before and thought, "Wow, I never saw that before. Has that always been in there? I don't ever remember seeing that"? That's part of how you know it's Scripture. Have you ever had that happen when reading any other book? That's not a coincidence. His Spirit is in His Word and He speaks directly to your heart through spending time in His Word.

Some of you may think, "If I just memorize enough Scripture I'll be there." But God says through David, "I have stored up your word in my heart, that I might not sin against you" (Psa. 119:11). There is nothing better than committing to heart memory what God says in His Word and letting it soak deeply into your soul. It nourishes your soul, it enlightens, and it produces wisdom. But it does require three distinct steps.

The enemy will try to stop you the minute you decide to take these steps.

Read It

Spend time in the Word and savor His words. I recommend asking God to show you what He has for you before you even start reading. After all, they are His words. Ask Him to open your eyes to what He wants to show you, even if it's not pretty. Sometimes His Word shines a spotlight on things we'd rather not see in ourselves. But we need that. We can't be honest with ourselves if we can't accept where we really are and ask Him to help us work on that area of character change. He is building the sword of the Spirit in your life.

Believe It

I can read and even understand what God is saying, but if I don't believe Him fully, it's just great words that don't fully apply to me. We may say, "I hear You, God, but You can't mean my heart is like that parable I read. That's for people who don't have mercy for others, and I always do. Or I think I do. I hope I do. Okay, maybe I don't always, but that's only because they don't deserve mercy. And I get to decide who gets mercy and who doesn't, right?" We must not only understand it, but we must believe that it applies to each of us, and know how it applies, or we won't do anything with it. Even if we have it memorized, He is building the sword of the Spirit in each of our lives.

> **The enemy will try to stop you the minute you decide to take these steps.**

Act on It

Only if I have read, understood, and believe what He says, and understand how it applies to me, will any of this make any difference. Have I asked him how He wants me to live this armor-plated existence out in my life? Knowing without believing is just raw knowledge. Not bad to have, but it can't impact my life or anyone else's if I don't act on it. If I really believe it, do I really believe Him? Remember, belief is from the heart, not just from the mind. I should feel urgency to put some of it into practice in my life and the lives of those around me. Only when His words have that kind of impact does it matter that I read and memorized His Word and put a plan together with the Holy Spirit to do something, build something, with what He has said. It's not what you know; it's what you do with what you know. He is building the sword of the Spirit in your life.

There are many, many ways to study the Word. It can be confusing and overwhelming if you are just getting started for the first time, or even trying to go back for another try after previous attempts. There are study Bibles, commentaries, Bible dictionaries, and study courses for individual books. The Internet is filled with all the above. Just remember, satan wants to discourage this behavior at all costs. Don't put too much stress on yourself. Christ said His yoke is easy and His burden is light. If it feels like a burden, you're doing it wrong.

Seriously, God wants to talk to you directly about Himself and about your story. He is not trying to confuse or frustrate you. Take a deep breath. He wants you to understand what He's saying to you. He wants to talk directly to your heart. A couple of cautions if you're a beginner. Don't start in Revelation. Start with a Gospel (Matthew, Mark, Luke, or John). Eventually, get into Romans and the rest of Paul's writings. It can all be part of the sword of the Spirit. Remember, "Faith comes from hearing, and hearing through the word of Christ" (Rom. 10:17).

Spirit Sword • 213

Don't forget the Old Testament. Psalms and Proverbs are good places to start. They are necessary reading. I was once in a session with Charles Ryrie just a few months before his death, and during the question-and-answer time, someone asked, what's the best version of the Bible? He said, "The one you'll read." You know the person that asked was trying to hear him say the version he was reading was the correct one. Don't put that kind of pressure on yourself or this process. Personal study is great, but your interest may start as part of a small group or Sunday school class.

If you then follow up on things you found interesting, or that you wanted to know more about, you can study it on your own. Over time you will build a library of topics that you didn't know were connected, and over time Scripture will coalesce into some key themes. This is the process of sword-building activity.

Know that God's heart is achieved by reading His Word and asking Him to apply it to your heart. That's what He wants. Ask Him for a passion to know Him and His Word and to talk with Him. You may be thinking, "But reading the Bible just doesn't interest me," or "I always get distracted and just can't spend much time praying." In James 4:2b (NIV), he says, "You do not have because you do not ask God."

If reading the Bible seems boring or uninspiring, ask Him for the desire to read and understand what He has written. Ask Him to help you understand it as you read it. It may sound simple, but it's often a step we leave out, and it's vital. Prayer should be your first step every time you read

His Word or talk to Him in prayer. Meaningful prayer is an intimate, two-way, ongoing conversation between you and the God of the universe. It is what He wants for you more than anything else. He wants to know you at a heart level, and these two methods, reading His Word and talking to Him, are the primary ways He speaks into all of us.

As you go out, moving into the lives of the others in your life, you carry with you this Word, to be used by the Spirit. He goes with you, residing in you, and will give you what you need for where you are and who you're with. Christ remembered what He believed and told satan so. And satan left. If we follow Christ, we become like Him. If we become like Him, we do what He does. He set captives free. In Luke 4:18, Jesus was reading from Isaiah 61:1–2, saying that he came to "proclaim liberty to the captives … to set at liberty those who are oppressed."

So, no matter where you go, you have the Word to offer:

> *For as the rain and the snow come down from heaven and do not return there but water the earth, making it bring forth and sprout, giving seed to the sower and bread to the eater, so shall my **word** be that goes out from my mouth; it shall not return to me empty, but it shall accomplish that which I purpose, and shall succeed in the thing for which I sent it.*
>
> (ISAIAH 55:10–11, EMPHASIS MINE)

The Sword Is an Offensive Weapon

The fact is, the sword is the key offensive tool.

The gates of hell are not

impermeable—it's just that

few people want to push

against them.

---

*The gates of hell are not impermeable—it's just
that few people want to push against them.*

Who wants to purposely get that close to evil? Who is armored up enough to go on rescue missions? We all should
be. More on that in the last chapter. God surely does want
us to push back against satan and his schemes. We don't
have to curl up and sit in a corner trying to defend ourselves. Romans 8:37 says, "No, in all these things we are
more than conquerors through him who loved us." Are
you?

He equips us to take on satan and not just run and hide. Are
you comfortable entering your world at that kind of disad-
vantage when you can start learning more about His Word
instead? Psalm 119:11 says, "I have hidden your word in
my heart that I might not sin against you." The Word has
power to enable you in several ways, including helping
you not to sin.

*And I tell you, you are Peter, and on this rock, I
will build my church, and the **gates of hell shall
not prevail** against it.*

(MATTHEW 16:18, EMPHASIS MINE)

Imagine the property lines that extend from the edges of
the gates of hell. Think of people currently living who are
behind those gates. These are captive prisoners of satan,
people who are still related to him. As we interact with
them, we must handle the Word well: "Do your best to
present yourself to God as one approved, a *worker* who
does not need to be ashamed and who correctly handles

the *word of truth*" (2 Tim. 2:15 NIV, emphasis mine). That is our sword.

There are people always around, everywhere you go. Those who follow Christ and those who do not. They always need a touch of Him, His Word. You carry Him, the Word, with you ... His love, His joy, His kindness, His peace, His patience, His goodness. People who are still captive behind the gates of hell need you to show them who Jesus is. Others are waiting on your obedience. You are to rescue them by whose you are and what you wear, your armor, which is Christ Himself. As you move forward with the sword in front of you, you are declaring who He is from His Word before arrows are shot against you. You show up as someone who *is His*—walking in salvation, peace, truth, right acts, right beliefs, and His Word. You should have the character traits of the One you follow.

Think of someone you might see next week who is anxious. Who do you know who is hopeless? Do you know anyone who will have very little joy in this season of life, or whatever they are going through? You can deliver those attributes to them even though they may be behind the gates or in a corner cowering. How does the Word move you forward? Do you know Jesus well enough to tell someone what He is like and how He has helped you? Using your own words, why not write that out so you can see what you might say. You don't need big words or Greek words, just your words. However, it might be you in the corner. There is no shame in admitting that. But you need someone to help you out of the corner. Go back to the "Sharine Shields" chapter. You may not be the one sharing a shield;

you may need someone to share their shield with you. Pray and ask God to show you who can help you.

Christ Himself will show up at the end of all things, and He will have a sword. His sword will be His words:

> *He is clothed in a robe dipped in blood, and the name by which he is called is The Word of God. And the armies of heaven, arrayed in fine linen, white and pure, were following him on white horses. From his mouth comes a sharp sword with which to strike down the nations....*
>
> *(REVELATION 19:13–15)*

He will push down all gates and end all principalities of the enemy. The only thing left will be for Him to cast satan, and those who follow him, into the lake of fire to reside forever.

Chapter 14

Righteous Breastplate

*...and having put on the breastplate of righteous-
ness....*

(EPHESIANS 6:14)

For those of you who believe in Christ (you have told
Him you believe in Him with your heart and that
He is Lord, according to Romans 10:9–10), you are
positionally completely righteous in Christ.

Let's unpack that a little.

Are you righteous enough today to get into heaven? That's
a big question. If you have accepted Christ's gift of salvation, the answer is yes. You're considered righteous
enough to enter God's presence just the way you are.

But, that's not because you're just a great person. It's because when God looks at you, He sees the righteousness
of Jesus and that makes you completely righteous. You enter heaven based on the righteousness you already have
through Jesus (not yours) and you will live forever with
Him, without any sin. You are deemed and declared righteous in God's eyes, but you don't always act righteous in
the eyes of others.

You might be asking, "If I'm ready to go right now, how can the sins that I still commit not count against me?" As Paul says, "I do not understand what I do. For what I want to do I do not do, but what I hate I do" (Rom. 7:15 NIV). If I'm already righteous enough for heaven, how can I still sin and still be ready at the same time? The problem is timing. What about the time from here to when I go to heaven, the sin I do between now and then? It seems inconsistent. Your sins have been forgiven from the past, the present, and any future sins.

Oh well, then I can sin, and it doesn't matter? Nope. Not according to Romans 6:1–4 (NIV):

> *What shall we say, then? Shall we go on sinning so that grace may increase? By no means! We are those who have died to sin; how can we live in it any longer? Or don't you know that all of us who were baptized into Christ Jesus were baptized into his death? We were therefore buried with him through baptism into death in order that, just as Christ was raised from the dead through the glory of the Father, we too may live a new life.*

First Corinthians 3:13–15 describes the judgment Christians will go through. The big word is the "*Bema* seat" judgment. All Christians will be a part of this. We will not be part of the "Great White Throne," the judgment for those that have rejected God's free gift. As believers, we cannot go to hell. But, as the end of this set of verses shows, some people may barely show that they are His, based on how they live their lives. How you live matters, even as a Christian. The verses in 1 Corinthians say:

*Their work will be shown for what it is, because
the Day will bring it to light. It will be revealed
with fire, and the fire will test the quality of each
person's work. If what has been built survives, the
builder will receive a reward. If it is burned up,
the builder will suffer loss but yet will be saved—
even though only as one escaping through the
flames.*

(1 CORINTHIANS 3:13–15 NIV)

You cannot get more righteous from here. No actions on
your part will make you any more righteous. But your right
thoughts and actions must consistently be growing. Those
right thoughts and actions represent that positional righteousness you have because of Christ.

"He put on righteousness as a breastplate, and a helmet of
salvation on his head; he put on garments of vengeance
for clothing, and wrapped himself in zeal as a cloak"
(Isa. 59:17 – prophecy speaking of Christ).

So, if you are a believer, a follower of Christ because you
have placed your faith in Him, you are positionally righteous. You could not pursue righteousness or have it increase if that were not the case. You can't clean up, then
come to Christ. You come to Christ, are forgiven, and then
He cleans up what has been entrusted to Him for forgiveness. In 1 John 1:9–10, God says, "If we confess our sins,
he is faithful and just to forgive us our sins and to cleanse
us from all unrighteousness. If we say we have not sinned,
we make him a liar, and his word is not in us."

God forgives us, then cleanses us of unrighteousness, and we become more righteous in our thoughts and actions, which change increasingly over time and match our positional righteousness.

We have it "in full," and yet it must increase "in what it is."

Righteousness is this: the quality of doing what God requires, and doing what is right. I can't think of another way to say that. We can all admit we don't do what is right all the time. We don't think what is right all the time. We don't always do all that we should all the time. We don't always respond as we should all the time. We all have some room to grow.

In a strange sort of way, you get "positional righteousness" as a starter kit. Complete, but being added to. You are positionally righteous in Christ. But your thoughts and actions which represent that righteousness looks more like a Mr. T starter kit … just medallions around your neck covering a very small portion of your chest (Mr. T – from *The A-Team*).

> *We have it "in full," and yet it must increase "in what it is."*

We should pursue it, train for it, hunger for it, and thirst for it. "Sanctification" is a word which fits here. We must *grow up* into who we are to be. Like Him. It is at times tough to understand that our righteousness was bought completely for us by Christ, but we must act it out. "For our sake he made him to be sin who knew no sin, so that in him we might become the *righteousness* of God" (2 Cor. 5:21, emphasis mine). In 2 Timothy 2:22, Paul tells Timothy to "flee youthful passions and *pursue righteousness, faith, love, and peace, along with those who call on the Lord from a pure heart*" (emphasis mine).

*All Scripture is breathed out by God and profitable for teaching, for reproof, for correction, and for **training in righteousness**, that the man of God may be complete, equipped for every good work.*

(2 TIMOTHY 3:16–17, EMPHASIS MINE)

*Blessed are those who **hunger and thirst for righteousness**, for they shall be satisfied.*

(MATTHEW 5:6, EMPHASIS MINE)

It is possible for us to not thirst for it. To not hunger for it. But we are blessed if we do. It is not possible to be totally filled this side of heaven. If it were, this would be heaven. Thank heaven it is not! This fallen world we live in is insatiable for the things of this world. But we who follow Christ are to be satiated only by the things of His kingdom. Righteousness is one of them.

In Romans 9:30–32a, Paul says:

*What shall we say, then? That Gentiles who did not pursue **righteousness** have attained it, that is, a **righteousness** that is by faith; but that Israel who pursued a law that would lead to **righteousness** did not succeed in reaching that law. Why? Because they did not **pursue it by faith**, but as if it were based on works. (emphasis mine)*

They did not believe Him. They just pursued correct actions as best they could with their own works.

Genesis 15:6, Romans 4:3, 5, 9, 11, 22, Galatians 3:6, and James 2:23, all speak of how *faith* was accounted to past saints as *righteousness.*

> *And he said to them, "Is a lamp brought in to be put under a basket, or under a bed, and not on a stand? For nothing is hidden except to be made manifest; nor is anything secret except to come to light."*
>
> *(MARK 4:21–22)*

> *Look carefully then how you walk, not as unwise but as wise, making the best use of the time, because the days are evil.*
>
> *(EPHESIANS 5:15–16)*

> *You have put off the old self with its practices and have put on the new self, which is **being renewed** in knowledge after the image of its creator.*
>
> *(COLOSSIANS 3:9–10, EMPHASIS MINE)*

> *You are one hundred percent righteous positionally, and yet you are to become more righteous (in your actions) each day.*

Positionally, God sees you as the righteousness of Christ, because of what Christ has done for you. So, He sees you as completely righteous! That will never change. Yet, in the eyes of the world, they see you changing daily to look more like whose you are. Righteousness is by faith. Then, it is to be actions (internal and external) which portray the righteous standing you have.

———————————

You are one hundred precent

righteous positionally, and

yet you are to become *more*

righteous (in your actions)

each day.

———————————

226 • Tiny Armor?

Right about now you are saying, "I'm exhausted having so many different Scriptures in a row thrown at me." The point here is for this to be a nail-it-down juncture. You must decide with your will that you will ask God to help you see where your actions do not match the righteousness He has given you, and ask Him to help you change your actions. Fasten securely all those verses on your breastplate. You can never know too much about Him! But, where you talk like Him, but don't look like Him, you'll look like a hypocrite. No one wants to be labeled that. Strive to have your actionable righteousness start moving toward looking like your positional righteousness.

You don't want those who know you to question your positional righteousness because of your un-right action. And we surely do not want to reveal something which is not true about Him.

We do not want to misrepresent Him.

But we do.

Daily.

Hourly.

In our mind and in our actions.

What do your visible actions tell others about whose you are? Who you follow? To the degree you do not act like the righteousness you have, you give Christ a black eye. It is your faith and belief in Christ and desire to follow Him that will change your actions. He is the One who can help you change.

*Right actions by faith do not cause **righteousness**. Right actions by faith prove that positional **righteousness** exists.*

Let's think about the first part of the quote. Right actions by faith do not cause righteousness. Righteous actions point to righteous position. It's just like what God says in James 2:17 (NIV), "In the same way, faith by itself, if it is not accompanied by action, is dead."

Maybe you have seen a veteran wearing his uniform with the war medals on the chests of their uniforms. Those medals represent the "right acts" they have done. They were already enlisted and had courage to be a soldier. Their medals represent their "right actions" as a soldier. They don't wear "right action" medals as a form of personal pride. But those medals point to a devotion they already had as a soldier, and then exemplified during battle.

Right actions by faith do not cause righteousness. Right actions by faith prove that positional righteousness exists.

Here is the great thing about having a breastplate of righteousness. Christ secured it for you and gave it to you. It is sealed and done and can't be taken away from you or destroyed. Just like your helmet of salvation. You just need to wear it well, with honor, as your righteous actions help you stand your ground and move forward for others, as well as point to where the righteousness came from … Christ. "For in it the righteousness of God is revealed from faith

for faith, as it is written, 'The righteous shall live by faith'"
(Rom. 1:17).

> *You believe (have faith) because of that truth you have, and you are to be "rightly working" (acting) based on that truth you deeply believe.*

You believe (have faith) because of that truth you have, and you are to be "rightly working" (acting) based on that truth you deeply believe.

What areas are there to grow in? What specific acts or deeds does righteousness entail? We must pursue righteousness, right living, so that we exhibit who He is and others can see the love and graciousness of the One who saved us.

There are basic areas where the righteousness of your breastplate can grow: in your mind, in your actions (unrighteousness that becomes more righteousness), and in the actions that you don't currently do, but should start. Within each of these categories, there are many relationships to which God speaks: moms, dads, children, coworkers, bosses, the government. All those we meet. All neighbors. Pretty much anyone. They are all watching.

Holes in Your Righteousness

When we think about the breastplate of righteousness, again we think more about the illustration than we do about what it illustrates. We think more about the look and the design of a breastplate than we do the righteousness it represents. Again, we don't get our righteousness fully formed, but we get it fully available. We have no holes in our positional righteousness because that is from Christ. But we have holes in our "righteous actions," because we don't always act out the righteousness that we have. We don't always think as we should or act as we should. We need to "walk by the Spirit, and you will not gratify the desires of the flesh" (Gal. 5:16). The Spirit will guide you to correct acting. I know I can sense Him correcting me as I'm contemplating an action. I am growing more accustomed to hearing His voice and sensing His guidance. But I still have gaping holes in my actions.

When we become His, we get a totally right-standing before God. We are positionally completely righteous in the eyes of God. We get sealed for the day of redemption. So, positionally, in God's eyes we are perfect. Yet we are at the same time becoming perfect in the eyes of others. Both are true at the same time, even though they seem to contradict each other. How can a person be perfect and also, at the same time, be getting perfect? Back again to 1 John 1:9 as God explains it: "If we confess our sins, he is faithful and just to *forgive us* our sins and to *cleanse us* from all unrighteousness" (emphasis mine). He is the One doing the forgiving and the cleansing. Also, in Romans 8:29, He says we are "...*to become* conformed to the image of his Son..." (emphasis mine). Our unrighteousness must decrease, and our righteousness will increase as we become more like Christ. He does both. But we must be willing participants.

In John 13:34–35, Jesus says, "A new commandment I give to you, that you love one another: just as I have loved you, you also are to love one another. By this all people will know that you are my disciples, if you have love for one another." Francis Schaeffer, in his book, *The Mark of the Christian,* comments about this verse: "In the midst of the world, in the midst of our present dying culture, Jesus is giving a right to the world. Upon his authority he gives the world the right to judge whether you and I are born-again Christians on the basis of our observable love toward all Christians."[6] Our righteous loving actions should be evident. Because it is the evidence that we are Christ's disciples. Is it more evident over time, to those around us, that we have positional righteousness because of Christ? Do our behaviors change for the better? Do we start having new actions we did not in the past? If you're brave enough, ask those closest to you about the holes in your righteous actions.

"Abraham believed God, and it was counted to him as righteousness" (Rom. 4:3). Positionally, Abraham was righteous and headed to heaven when he died. It was a done deal and decided. It was "counted to him." But even Abraham had issues in his life.

"You therefore must *be perfect*, as your heavenly Father *is perfect*. Beware of practicing your righteousness before other people in order to be seen by them, for then you will have no reward from your Father who is in heaven" (Matt. 5:48–6:1). Two verses back to back. This break between chapters can give us some issues of understanding. But there is no chapter break in the original manuscripts.

6   Schaeffer, Francis A. *The Mark of the Christian.* (Downers Grove, IL: 2006).

Breaks of chapters and verses were added in the 1200s. We are to "be becoming perfect" and, at the same time, beware of practicing righteousness in front of others so they will notice us. And yet, in Matthew 5:16, it says, "In the same way, let your light shine before others, so that they may see your good works and give glory to your Father who is in heaven." Our right actions should be visible to others and they should thank God for them.

God is already perfect, and always has been. The type of verb is a "present verb," which means "is right now." For us, it's a "future verb." Better said, we are to "be becoming perfect" as God is now and always has been perfect. Two different verb tenses here. God is, and we are becoming. Change must happen in our lives. Active righteousness must increase. In God's mind we are already thought of as complete, and just waiting to arrive home. Here on earth, during the rest of our lives, change must happen so that others see more and more of who God is in our lives. These two thoughts on perfection and righteousness are purposely tied together as we become more like Christ.

When Paul was inspired by God to write to Timothy the second time, he included this statement: "All Scripture is breathed out by God and profitable for teaching, for reproof, for correction, and for training in righteousness, that the man of God may be complete, equipped for every *good work*" (2 Tim. 3:16–17, emphasis mine). The idea in this verse is that you can learn and get better at being righteous in your thoughts and actions. Your thoughts and actions matter!

It is His righteousness we are wearing, not ours. Paul said:

> For his sake I have suffered the loss of all things
> and count them as rubbish, in order that I may
> gain Christ and be found in him, **not having a**
> **righteousness of my own** that comes from the law,
> but that which comes through faith in Christ, the
> righteousness from God that depends on faith.
>
> (PHILIPPIANS 3:8B–9, EMPHASIS MINE)

Just as our faith (shield) must increase, and we must work out our salvation (helmet). Our righteousness is something we have full possibility of, but we must pursue it. We must run after correct living and acting. Again, I have to realize that a breastplate is offered to me. It is one hundred percent effective, but I must wear it one hundred percent correctly and one hundred percent of the time. The holes show up in many ways when I don't know what righteousness is. Again, you cannot wear what you do not know. When I choose not to wear it, and when I wear it improperly, I am acting un-righteously.

Martin Luther said, "Be careful not to measure your holiness by other people's sins."[2] Too much of the time I am afraid that we judge ourselves by comparison with others. Either we sin more or less than someone else. Either our sin is worse, or not as bad as someone else. Thinking, "At least I'm more righteous than them," sounds more like a Pharisee than a follower of Christ.

In James 4:17 (NIV), God says, "If anyone, then, knows the good they ought to do and doesn't *do it,* it is sin for them" (emphasis mine). God can be asking you to do something. He could be putting something on your heart to do, or someone on your heart to talk to. If you don't do that, it is sin to you, not to me. I have my own things He has asked me to do. My righteousness must grow toward matching the righteousness given me by Christ. This will not be accomplished till death.

When my righteousness is only a fact or a state of mind which does not become a thought and an action, the armor has a potential hole. When I don't know what it is in a certain area of life, I will not be able to use it. What I don't know, I don't know, and can't use. But, when we live or act according to His standard, His life, we are using His righteousness properly.

We must know it exists, who it came from, and how to use it.

So, get to know the One who offers you His righteousness.

He will explain His righteousness and how to use it.

Chapter 15

Peaceful Sandals

...and, as shoes for your feet, having put on the readiness given by the gospel of peace.

(EPHESIANS 6:15)

"Peaceful Sandals" sounds like a shoe brand designed by hippies in the sixties. But, the Prince of Peace wears them. And "peaceful readiness" is one of the attributes He brings to us in the midst of war and anxiety. On the day of His resurrection, that evening, Jesus just shows up in the midst of the disciples—the disciples who were behind locked doors for fear of the Jews who had just had Him killed. Through the wall Jesus just shows up. The first thing He says? "Peace be with you" (John 20:19). John records this in John 20:19–20: "On the evening of that day, the first day of the week, the doors being locked where the disciples were for fear of the Jews, Jesus came and stood among them and said to them, 'Peace be with you.'"

Then He says it again. "Jesus said to them again, 'Peace be with you. As the Father has sent me, even so I am sending you'" (John 20:21).

Why repeat it? Because they were scared. They thought He was a ghost. And they feared the Jews. But then Jesus also said, "I am sending you."

This is why we must be ready to be sent and be peaceful as we go. Those you interact with are also at war, and probably have little peace. You might be a bit low on peace, or on empty after these last few years. The world around us can seem chaotic, out of control, and increasingly unkind.

In 2022, war in Ukraine got everyone's attention and added another layer of fear around the world—which was just what we needed after COVID-19. Political strife. Racial strife. These invaded our worlds. There are increasingly smaller places to hide from the encroachment around us. The impacts to our mental, emotional, and spiritual health are enormous. As a people, we really need peace. We need His peace.

Those without Christ have no peace within or without. No peace deep in their soul, and no peace in their lives. Honestly, I wonder what keeps them going.

And Christians are not immune from the effects of these issues if we don't keep our focus in the right place and keep our perspective. That's what we lose first when problems hit— perspective. We lose our frame of reference, and we can overact and lose the sense of our core principles because of an emotional response to things happening around us. Christians are not exempt.

"Do not think that I have come to bring peace to the earth. I have not come to bring peace, but a sword" (Matt. 10:34). Don't get concerned about this verse and how you apply it. He did not come to bring peace to the earth, but He does want to bring you peace in the midst of a non-peaceful place. In the end times, He will bring that final peace. For now, He is focused on those who love Him, choose to follow Him, and are building armor of Him.

But, "Blessed are the peacemakers, for they shall be called sons of God" (Matt. 5:9). We must be ready to be these peacemakers. Preparation, ability, and resolution is what the word for readiness means. We must show up, ready as asked, with peace. And we must go when we are asked. The prophet Isaiah tells us that it is God who can keep us peaceful. But our minds must be stayed on Him, not our circumstances or incoming arrows. "You keep him in perfect peace whose mind is stayed on you, because he trusts in you" (Isa. 26:3). When we show up, anywhere in our lives, we should be wearing the sandals of the "readiness" of the gospel of peace. Not just the gospel, but the gospel of peace because of our relationship with Him.

Too much of the time I think we misunderstand the gospel. It literally means "good news." The apostle Mark says in Mark 1:1, "The beginning of the gospel of Jesus Christ, the Son of God." It is the beginning of the good news. We are to carry it forward.

We are to be peacemakers: makers of peace. There is no need to make peace if peace already exists. But, in the midst of any level of calamity, He sends us to deliver peace. But we must already have peace. We must be prepared. "'For the mountains may be removed and the hills may shake, but My favor will not be removed from you, nor will My covenant of peace be shaken,' says the LORD who has compassion on you" (Isa. 54:10 NASB). Isaiah knew God's peace. And he showed up peaceful in tough situations, with peace to give to whomever, and wherever, God sent him.

And in Philippians 4, God tells us that we can trade anxiety for peace. What a deal! But most of the time we don't. Look at what God says about peace in Philippians 4:5–7:

> *The Lord is at hand; do not be anxious about anything, but in everything by prayer and supplication with thanksgiving let your requests be made known to God. And the **peace of God**, which surpasses all understanding, will guard your hearts and your minds in Christ Jesus. (emphasis mine)*

Here Is the Shift We Must Make

Every time we see the word "gospel," we need to think "good news." That is the best translation of the Greek word *euangelion*. The gospel of Jesus Christ is the good news of Jesus Christ. What is the first good news which people in distress need? Peace. In the illustration of the armor, the good news is "peace with God," and "God as your peace." The sandals of Ephesians 6:15 are "peace:" "And, as shoes for your feet, having

Be ready when the Spirit prompts your spirit (taps you on the shoulder) and says go, so that you go with peace.

put on the readiness given by the gospel of peace." If our sandals are on, we show up with the good news of peace. Much of the time, those we meet know there is a war going on in their soul, and they are attempting to medicate it with the things of this world. They are not sure what to do with it all. You yourself have done this. And you needed peace.

Be ready when the Spirit prompts your spirit (taps you on the shoulder) and says go, so that you go with peace.

We must be ready and prepared to go at a moment's notice. No one needs you to show up to help them if you are not peaceful. If you are anxious, angry, and unsettled, you'll not be bringing peace to that situation. You'll probably bring more anxiety, more anger, and an unsettled nature. Most likely those things already exist where you are sent. What people need is the peace Christ offers. Handwringing and furrowed brows don't inspire confidence in people around you, or the One you say you follow. That will not inspire them to ask about the hope within you. There won't be any hope to ask about. In fact, they may ask if you want a drink to calm down. You'll look no different from the world around you.

You must *have* the good news of peace to be prepared to *offer* the good news of peace. In many cases I know I have shown up to help barefooted…. No peace.

Back to the part about Him sending us. In Luke 10:5–6 (NASB), "Whatever house you enter, first say, 'Peace be to this house.' If a man of peace is there, your peace will rest on him; but if not, it will return to you." Jesus will send us. And as we go about our lives, we are not just to bring peace, but to look for those who have peace and partner with them, and allow our peace to grow.

But there are some people who just will not allow peace in their lives. We may offer it. We may want badly to see them peaceful … but they just won't have it. At that point it is impossible to fight *for* them because you are actually fighting *against* them. Anxious people do not portray trust in God. This again is one reason God made sure Paul said to put on the whole armor of God. Because we will look pitiful half-dressed for battle. Like running barefoot through a briar patch. Just not smart. So, don't walk around barefooted anxiously trying to share a gospel without peace.

You lead with peace!

Preparation/Readiness and Peace Are Vitally Important

Mark likes to hike twenty-four miles across the Grand Canyon in one day. Called "rim-to-rim," he has done it seven times now. Doug has done it with him on two of those occasions.

He tends to get one of two reactions when the topic comes up in conversation. Either…

- That's the dumbest thing I've ever heard.
- That sounds terrible.
- Why would anyone want to do that?

The other is…

- Wow.
- That's cool.
- I want to go on that trip!
- Can you take me with you the next time you go?

And yes, there are more people who adhere to the first belief than the second.

Unfortunately, the people who want to go typically don't have much of a clue about what it takes to be ready for a hike like this. Some have said, "I know I can make it because my wife and I walk around the block a lot." It's hard not to sound like a hiking snob when you ask them how many days a week they go to the gym. Sometimes Mark hears, "Oh, I don't go to the gym. We walk instead." He tries to, as diplomatically as possible, help them understand he would never go with them in this lifetime and be responsible for their demise in that amazing paradise.

It's hard not to laugh at what some think this hike is like. They think it's a neat concept and they're enamored with the romance of it all. But they don't think through what it really takes to be ready. There are three levels of completion, assuming you do complete it (that's not assured—ask Doug, we had a couple of adventures on our two trips):

- Level One is to finish the trip and collapse at the top of the trailhead and say, "That was the dumbest thing I've ever done. I'm never doing that again, but I can mark it off my bucket list."
- Level Two says, "I will decide after breakfast tomorrow if I'm ever coming back. I might."
- Level Three is when you hit the top and put in your phone the date for the next time you plan to come back.

Mark has seen all three levels in his hiking companions, and Level One is not pretty.

There are about 650 people per summer that are extracted from inside the canyon by park officials. That's not really because of people doing rim-to-rim. It's just people from flatlands and cities showing up at a pretty place to hike a little. Mark says, "And, of course, you wouldn't believe what I've seen. People walking two or three miles down in the canyon in late August with flip-flops, no food, and no water. I've encountered some of these folks in 120 degree heat, and asked those red-faced adventurers, 'So, how far do you plan to hike?' As the blood ran from beneath the toes of their flip-flops, most often the answer was that they planned to walk until they got tired, and then they would turn around and walk back up."

It takes a lot of diplomacy not to roll your eyes as you ask them to think about what they just said. "So, you're going to walk even further in these conditions, for which you are clearly not prepared, until you are tired … and then expect to get up the four miles you have already hiked down, going up, in this heat while gaining altitude with no food or water and bleeding between your toes?" Yes, it is harder going up than down, *except* on your knees and ankles, which is worse going down. You wonder how it's possible for people to be this clueless about what is going to happen to them. This is not what preparedness looks like.

Again, I'm not even talking about people doing rim-to-rim—just regular folks on one- or two-mile hikes that are part of that 650 people per summer that have to get rescued. And, by the way, there are usually about a dozen deaths a year at the Grand Canyon, most of them by people taking that one extra step for the perfect picture, and never getting to see that picture.

Some are hauled out by mule. Some are extracted by helicopter. That's a quick $5,000 if you have the foresight to be lifted out during the day. It's a $20,000 trip if they get you out at night. Think military extraction. Night vision goggles, people rappelling down a rope on the side of a major incline as they strap you to the person getting you and lift you into the helicopter. Or it could be more serious, and they must get you on a gurney and lift you to that helicopter before they transport you to a hospital one hundred miles away. You don't call them for just a blister. Although if you have a blister for twenty-four miles, you may feel like you need an emergency helicopter. Doug and I have seen this helicopter extraction on one of our hikes. That's how we know about how much it costs.

The enemy would love to keep you so unprepared that you have to be carried off the battlefield, never to return.

One of the best examples of not planning, or being prepared well, was on the normal six-hour van ride going around from the South Rim to the North Rim where we would begin our one-day sojourn the following morning. There is good reason to spend $90 to do this so you can trek North to South. If you go from the South Rim to the North Rim, when you finish the trek, you are still three miles from the lodge where there is civilization. If you go North to South, you hit the top of the rim and your cabin is

_____

The enemy would love to keep you so unprepared that you have to be carried off the battlefield, never to return.

_____

two hundred feet away from the trail head, as is the restaurant, with some more food and, more importantly, seats to sit on after a fourteen-hour day of walking in God's amazing beauty. Guess which one we pick?

On one of the van rides, the topic of the hike came up and they discovered I had done the trip five other times. A few of them were going to attempt rim-to-rim in one day, like me, the following day. They inquired what the trip was like. I was trying to be as nice as possible knowing it was too late to get any more prepared than they already were. One group said, "Well, I've heard from a friend it's only a four-hour hike, and we have a flight out tomorrow afternoon." They were believing a lie. I gently said, "I would reschedule your flight. You won't even be out of the canyon by your flight time." They continued to insist that "their friend," who had never been on the trip, but had "researched it," was right and it was really a four-hour trip. I said, "Your friend is wrong, but good luck." They did subsequently plan to leave an hour earlier because of my negative view of their four-hour forecast. I said there would be a "four" in the time the trek takes, but it would be preceded by a "one" ... making it a fourteen-hour trip. I just left it at that. They just would not believe me.

After that, the gentleman behind me said, "I heard what you told those people. You make this trip sound hard." Remember, I was trying to be honest, but with a little grace mixed in so they could at least sleep that evening. I said, "Well, it is." The look on his face was priceless. He then said, "You make it sound like you need special shoes or something, like tennis shoes or hiking shoes." I assured him that was true. I could not believe what I was hearing.

The look on his face became a distant stare as he processed what I was saying. He said, "I'm walking with a client and some coworkers, and at the end of the hike we will sign a big contract on the South Rim." He said that they had sent him some emails about how he should probably workout some to be ready, but he didn't have time to do that, or even really read the emails. Whoops. It was now fully hitting him what was ahead. He said, "All I brought was a suit and my wing-tipped shoes for the signing." I'm not sure what my face looked like, but I can only imagine it didn't inspire confidence in his predicament.

> *You don't wear wing-tipped dress shoes to hike the Grand Canyon.*

I very firmly said, "Do you see our van driver? If you want to be at that signing, you should give him another $90 to take you back around to the South Rim tomorrow morning." He seemed stunned, so I had said enough. There are no options for getting shoes, etc., on the remote North Rim. You're one hundred miles from any civilization and further from specialized hiking shoes. To this day, I don't know what he ultimately did.

The group that left on the hike an hour earlier than I did, I met the next afternoon three miles from the top of the South Rim. They were not having any fun and I didn't need to point out that they had missed their flight already and they had three miles to go. It was tough to listen as I filled up my water bottle. These three friends, from different parts of the country, who do something adventurous together every year, were severely berating their friend for not doing her homework on this trip and causing all their misery. Not prepared. It was something along the lines of, "You will never get to pick the destination again."

I'm pretty sure it's not the first time those words were said that day. Let's just say there was no peace in this non-prepared situation. I didn't have the heart to tell them the last

You don't wear wing-tipped dress shoes to hike the Grand Canyon.

three miles ahead of them were by far the hardest of the entire trip. I wished them well on their trip as I headed up. I thought it best not to say anything about the quality of the research their friend had done on the trip. I didn't need to.

They had believed lies, and wow, did the missing truth matter in that situation. More so in our souls when life is tough. And life can be tougher than just a bad day at the Grand Canyon. They can recover from that experience easier than job loss, or the loss of loved ones, or broken relationships, or any of the other things that can rob us of peace if we aren't prepared.

Flip-flops and wing-tipped shoes are great in the right context.

If you're at the beach, flip-flops are wonderful. If you're safely in the beautiful restaurant, signing a contract, wingtips are completely appropriate. Halfway down a dusty, twenty-four-mile arduous trail is not the place for either.

Know the terrain you're going to be traversing before you begin your journey each morning.

The right equipment, armor growing, is imperative for the battle ahead. There is no replacement for readiness.

Be prepared.

Be peaceful.

Show up.

Chapter 16

Truth Belt

*Stand firm therefore, having girded your loins with **truth**.*

(EPHESIANS 6:14, EMPHASIS MINE)

It is vitally important to know that you believe in "truth." And when each of us finds truth which we actually believe in, we need to make certain that it is truth. Does it line up with the Person who is truth? Each piece of the armor that is a part to the whole armor must be truth, and that is Christ. But, and this is a big "but," we've said it before, and here it is again: it is possible for you to know something with your mind, and not yet believe it in your heart.

Read that again.

Remember, the demons know who Christ is; they just don't believe Him. And don't believe in Him. They do not have faith in Christ, though they know and believe He exists. But they have faith in satan, and believe him.

How to Build a Truth Belt

As with the other pieces of armor, you must build it. It will not build itself. God will present truth to you daily—through His written Word (see John 17:17), through circumstances (see John 5:17), through other believers (see Ephesians 4:15–16), and through the Spirit revealing truth to you (see John 16:13). But, are you actively looking for truth?

You can ask Him daily: "Father, show me Your truth today." He will. The question is, "Will you hear it, see it, believe it, and incorporate it on to your belt, and the way you live your life?"

Truth is not what you choose to believe.

His truth is truth whether you believe it or not.

But, knowing it and believing it makes it part of your belt.

What you put on your belt must be true truth—spiritual truth that matters. You may believe that photosynthesis exists and that is how a tree grows. But, though that is true, it does not need to be a part of your belt. Yes, God created it that way, and you can and should believe that as truth. Reserve portions of your belt for the truth that is relational and actionable between the Trinity and yourself.

Knowing Truth versus Believing Truth

You probably have knowledge right now on your belt, but you have not used that knowledge on your shield. That's not good! Remember, it is the shield that extinguishes the flaming arrows, not the belt. The enemy does not want you to *know* any truth. And he also does not want you to *believe* that truth. He would even be okay with you knowing, but not believing. He would rather get stuff stuck in your head, but never your heart. You can believe truth, and not act on it. "You believe that God is one; you do well. *Even the demons believe*—and *shudder*! Do you want to be shown, you foolish person, that faith apart from works is useless?" (Jas. 2:19–20, emphasis mine). The demons know the truth, but they shudder to think about it. But disciples confess the truth (see Romans 10:9–10).

You have to put truth into action.

If you do find and know (mentally) some truth, the enemy will even do what he can to keep it only on the belt. That foe will never let you actually believe it, and then place that belief/faith in that truth on your shield and use it to stop the flaming arrows. The facts you know *about* God, Jesus, and the Holy Spirit, and Their ways, are true facts. But truth unapplied becomes useless facts. The demons have facts.

Truth unapplied becomes useless facts to you.

That hurts. Truth, but useless. Just like ointment not applied to poison ivy. It is useless while it's in the bottle. The truths below are useless to you if you do not apply them.

What God Says

God is big and powerful; He created everything (see Colossians 1:16).

He sees and knows everything and can do anything (see Isaiah 55:9; Hebrews 4:13; Ephesians 3:20).

He has always been that way (see Psalm 90:1–2).

Truth unapplied becomes

useless facts to you.

He "'is the Alpha and the Omega,' says the Lord God, 'who is and who was and who is to come, the Almighty'" (Rev. 1:8).

He cares about each of us (see Matthew 10:29–31).

He loves us, no matter what, even to the point of laying down His life for ours (see John 3:16).

He wants to spend time with us and for us to know Him (see Revelation 3:20).

He protects us and helps us and never moves (see 2 Thessalonians 3:3).

We may *know* all that, but do we *believe* all that? If you know it, but don't believe it, it is barely on your belt, and definitely not a part of your shield.

Things satan Says

God didn't create everything; it is all evolution. Even if God did create some version of processes for adaptation of it all … it was still not by His design.

God doesn't know or keep track of everything, and much of what is happening in the world is out of His control … and you are subject to the pain of what is still yet to come.

God will change His mind about you. You may think He loves you … but just wait.

God didn't really send His Son to die. That is a just a fable. A good one, but just a fable. Jesus was a good man. But just a man.

God has no time for you. He's too busy with major things. You don't really matter to Him. He just puts up with your antics in life.

God does not protect you. Remember when that horrible thing happened to you?

You don't have what it takes. God made you inferior to others.

Why even try? This whole planet is going to hell quickly. What difference can you make?

The enemy will tell you things like this daily. If you do not know truth (Jesus) and then believe truth (Jesus), the flaming arrows will hit your soul daily. But you *can* believe. The offer is there. He is waiting on you to acknowledge that He is King of Kings and Lord of Lords, and He is powerful and will be powerful for you. But you must armor up, and get the shield built and ready for arrows.

Jesus IS truth. "Jesus said to him, 'I am the way, and the *truth*, and the life. No one comes to the Father except through me. If you had known me, you would have known my Father also. From now on you do know him and have seen him'" (John 14:6–7, emphasis mine). Be obedient to Christ's truth.

Truth is a person—Christ.

Not an abstract fact.

So, *who* you don't know, can hurt you. And since the Spirit is with you always, He will guide you into all truth.

"When the Spirit of *truth* comes, he will guide you into all the *truth*, for he will not speak on his own authority, but whatever he hears he will speak..." (John 16:13, emphasis mine).

The Spirit will remind you of what you already know that Jesus has said.

> *If anyone loves me, he will keep my word, and my Father will love him, and we will come to him and make our home with him. Whoever does not love me does not keep my words. And the word that you hear is not mine but the Father's who sent me. These things I have spoken to you while I am still with you. But the Helper, the Holy Spirit, whom the Father will send in my name, he will teach you all things and bring to your remembrance all that I have said to you.*
>
> *(JOHN 14:23–26)*

So, what truths can you state right now that Jesus said? We all have small lists and tiny armor. What you don't know cannot be brought to your memory. But you can ask the Spirit to teach you new things which can be added to that list of what you know—then into belief in your heart—and be useful on your faith shield.

Truth versus Lies

What you don't know will harm you, and probably is harming you right now. And what you do know, you actually may know wrongly. Make sure what you know is *true truth*. Take every thought captive and subject it to truth—to Him.

> *For though we walk in the flesh, we are not waging war according to the flesh. For the weapons of our warfare are not of the flesh but have divine power to destroy strongholds. We destroy arguments and every lofty opinion **raised against the knowledge of God**, and **take every thought captive to obey Christ**, being ready to punish every disobedience, when your obedience is complete.*
> (2 CORINTHIANS 10:3–6, EMPHASIS MINE)

We must believe in the One who always stated truth, and is truth. As we've said, it is not just belief in a fact, but in the Person who IS truth.

> *Now faith is the assurance of things hoped for, the conviction of things not seen. For by it the people of old received their commendation. By faith we understand that the universe was created by the word of God, so that what is seen was not made out of things that are visible.*
> (HEBREWS 11:1–3)

Knowing truth ... is in a Person. The Person of Christ. What truth you know about Him is part of your belt. You believe that truth and also build your shield of belief/faith with that same truth.

We have faith in truth. Christ is right now who He said He was back then. The One we believe in, Jesus, is the second person of the Trinity. And as such, He said, "Whoever has seen me has seen the Father" (John 14:9). Jesus basically was the great I AM in person, up close and personal with all those He was ever near. He is now up close and in person to you, and available to you to wear as armor. He is the One who will walk you through the valley of the shadow of death, while you fear no evil (see Psalm 23:4). It is truth that He has already defeated death, so He only now has to walk you through the shadow death makes. Make no mistake—life can be fearful at any turn. But you are wearing the One, the truth, the Person who killed death. You do not have to believe the fearful lies of the enemy, that he is the one who holds your life in his hands, and that he has the final say on death. He does not. Christ does.

The truth, the whole truth, and nothing but the truth. satan has none of these three ... but ... Jesus IS ALL three of these.

Knowing truth ... is in a Person. The Person of Christ. What truth you know about Him is part of your belt. You believe that truth and also build your shield of belief/faith with that same truth.

Truth exposes the lies and schemes (attacks/arrows) the enemy is telling you. Increasingly get to know the truth about the One you believe in to counter the lies. What lies or half-truths are the enemy telling you? And which ones are you believing?

My Truth

"My truth" is a current label we use. That is the label of a movement prevalent in the twenty-first century. It says, "I get to determine what I believe. I get to determine what truth is, and you can't tell me I'm wrong. You can have

258 • *Tiny Armor?*

your truth, but you don't get to tell me what truth is for me."

We can each have what we call truth, but truth will come out in the end. Truth prevails, though you may have to live under the umbrella of someone's non-truth. That applies to governments, and other people, and God, and Scripture as well. I get to define truth for myself and for me that's valid. Each of us does, but many place validity on non-truth. It assumes that we can possess truth separate from a standard or any other construct that might impose a view on us. Jeremiah 17:9 pretty much sums up this thought process: "The heart is deceitful above all things, and desperately sick; who can understand it?" We have come by it honestly. Born into it. And we want to oversee all areas of our lives. Until we have a new heart, we use the old one.

As a society we've moved to a point where many genuinely believe that we get to determine what is right and wrong for ourselves ... and no other views need to be considered.

Logic, one of the staple concepts about a debated issue, is that one side can be right, and both can be wrong. But they can't both be right, or true. How do we determine truth in a world that says there is no standard and I get to decide what truth I follow?

But, of course, there are some standards imposed by society. You can't say you think it's fine to kill someone, and therefore it's okay to believe that and do it. We aren't to that point yet, but you can see how over time a society could be. The concept of personal truth is not new. It's

---

As a society we've moved

to a point where many

genuinely believe that we get

to determine what is right

and wrong for ourselves …

and no other views need to be

considered.

---

been around in various forms for quite a while. It was originally called relativism. But truth is not relative, no matter how much we might say it is.

Here's a very brief history of relativism. It was an outgrowth of the Enlightenment period of the seventeenth and eighteenth centuries, also known as the Age of Reason. Georg Wilhelm Friedrich Hegel, in the late 1700s, also played a major role in getting relativism entrenched in society. It has taken root deeply in our society now after a couple of centuries of development.

You can see the corrosive effects of that belief. Doesn't *relativism* sound like the kind of terrain on which satan would like to conduct spiritual warfare? You bet it does. We are deceived from the beginning, and we want to be in control of everything—just like in the Garden of Eden. So then we have this philosophical underpinning that feeds that natural human state of being deceived to the point we can't see how deceived we are. A lie now stands as truth. It's insidious.

Of course, if you think this little obstacle is too big for God to overcome, you may have tiny armor.

You're easy prey.

Bill Maher and "Jesus'"

A friend of mine from Florida, Les Cheveldayoff, was being interviewed by Bill Maher during the filming of a promotional segment for the film, *Religulous* (2008.) Les had been playing the part of Jesus at the *Holy Land Experience* in Orlando. And he did a great job. He looks more like Jesus than the pictures in Sunday school rooms. Also, Les is well over six feet tall, so he stands out quite a bit. Les was also in one of our Life Groups and the choir at First Baptist Church of Orlando.

Well, Bill Maher was interviewing him while Les was in full costume as Jesus. Bill asked a couple of funny questions like, "Do people come up to you in the lunch line and say … 'Lord'??? And do people stare at you?" Les said, "Trust me, they do!" Then Bill leaned in a little bit with his microphone and said, "Do you believe all this is true? What if you're wrong?" And then Les leaned down, even closer, looked Bill in the eyes and said, "What if you're wrong?" Bill froze for a moment. That interview was part of a TV commercial for a few days in Orlando. Then that portion of the commercial with Les was edited out. I wonder why? Because Les nailed him.

Any one of us can sincerely believe non-truth.

And we are sincerely wrong.

Part of what we do with apologetics is the ability to defend or explain the truth of God. But just because we can explain something well doesn't mean it's true. What God says is true, whether we believe it or can explain it well. Yet 1 Peter 3:15 (NASB) reminds us that, "always being ready to make a defense to everyone who asks you to give an account for the hope that is in you, yet with gentleness and reverence."

262 • *Tiny Armor?*

All That You Know Is Not True, and There Are Truths You Don't Know

All of what you believe about God is not true.

I guarantee if we could sit for a while and talk, we could find something you wholeheartedly believe is true, but is not. Something you believe is false. We all have these false beliefs. We attribute something to God which is just not true. Then we run our lives based on them.

Things like, "God helps those who help themselves." That is not in the Bible and bases His works solely on ours. You know what you know, but your knowledge is limited.

You must grow your knowledge of Him.

He wants you to.

He has taken the initiative. "For since the creation of the world His invisible attributes, that is, His eternal power and divine nature, have been clearly perceived, being understood by what has been made, so that they are without excuse" (Rom. 1:20 NASB).

He has been trying to show us who He is since He started.

We are the ones who just don't notice.

Chapter 17

Let's Cause a Problem in Hell

*...praying at **all times** in the Spirit, with **all prayer and supplication**. To that end keep alert with **all perseverance**, making supplication for all the saints, and also for me, that **words may be given** to me in opening my mouth **boldly to proclaim** the **mystery of the gospel**, for which I am an ambassador in chains, that I may **declare it boldly**, as **I ought to speak**.*

(EPHESIANS 6:18–20, EMPHASIS MINE)

The armor is not just for you. It is for you AND for you to rescue others.

As we grow our suit of armor, it's not just for our protection. The armor protects us while we go rescue and protect others. It's to protect us, but not only us. But rescue is much tougher if you have tiny armor yourself. That is why you need to use the sword of the Spirit as an offensive weapon. We are not saying you should intentionally decide to go after satan. But, when we do attempt to rescue and protect

> **The armor is not just for you. It is for you AND for you to rescue others.**

others, that causes a problem in hell. Our rescue operations mess up their plans on the whiteboards. The enemy will not like it.

Never Try to Build Armor Alone. Never!

Here's how it all works together. We develop our armor, and build our suit. And as you've read earlier, there are other people sharing a shield with us and praying for us, and going to battle alongside us, all while we are building and going about our lives.

We do the same for them.

We're meant for each other.

When the Pharisees asked Jesus what was the greatest commandment, He answered:

> *You shall love the Lord your God with all your heart and with all your soul and with all your mind. This is the great and first commandment. And a second is like it: You shall **love your neighbor as yourself**. On these two commandments depend all the Law and the Prophets.*
>
> *(MATTHEW 22:37–40, EMPHASIS MINE)*

You love yourself enough to read this book, and build a suit. So, love someone else enough, who is obviously spiritually naked, to help them build their suit. Be their prayer covering. Tell them how you built your suit. Tell them Jesus loves you and loves them and will save them and set them free (helmet). Tell them what you truly believe about Him (shield). Show them what right living/right actions look like (breastplate) and be peaceful when you are with them (shoes). And tell them the truth about all of this (belt). As you are doing this you are actually wielding the Word of God (sword). All that you have told them are things you now have as part of your armor which you can share with them. It's "the sword of the Spirit, which is the word of God" (Eph. 6:17). Your words and actions should match the *Word* of God.

> *In the beginning was the Word, and the **Word** was with God, and the **Word** was God. He was in the beginning with God. All things were made through him, and without him was not any thing made that was made. In him was life, and the life was the light of men. The light shines in the darkness, and the darkness has not overcome it.*
>
> (*JOHN 1:1–5, EMPHASIS MINE*)

All things were made through Him, even armor. You are overcoming darkness with your armor made of Him.

So, since Jesus is all parts of your armor, the darkness will not overcome Him. The armor of God is our covering and our protection as we move forward to rescue others who are captive. We are only doing what Jesus told us He was to do in Luke 4: "Set captives free." Your prayers and your bold movement forward cause problems with the plans the enemy has on the whiteboard. And because of that he and his henchmen may up their game against you. Be ready. Armor on. Shield up. Sword forward. You are moving further into enemy territory.

Paul prayed for us to pray, at ALL times, with ALL prayer and supplication, for ALL the saints. That now includes

ALL of us in the instruction. He is talking and praying always with the One who IS the armor. Talking to your Father, His Son, and the Spirit who leads you. That prayer is the same for us as it was for him, and for them. Paul's prayer to *boldly proclaim* and *declare boldly* is not just for street corners, pulpits, and "John 3:16" signs at football games. It is your life with others in your life.

One of the hardest things to realize is that God is not asking all of us to be preachers. He is asking all of us to be willing to humbly say what needs to be said and done for the sake of others. To love our neighbors, or whomever, to be truthful about who we know and what He is like. To tell the truth about the Word.

Do not fear. We are all to pray that we will all move forward boldly proclaiming the mystery of the gospel. What we say and how we act in any given situation should carry the weight of the Word. As we do this, we cause problems in hell, and hell pushes back as much as possible. He surely does not want us to move forward into occupied territory and set captives free.

We are all to be involved in boldly proclaiming and declaring. But we fear the wrong person many times. God says in Matthew 10:27–28, "What I tell you in the dark, say in the light, and what you hear whispered, *proclaim* on the housetops. And do not fear those who kill the body but cannot kill the soul. Rather fear him who can destroy both soul and body in hell" (emphasis mine).

Paul prayed that "words be given." And since his prayer is for all the saints, and that now includes us, we too must ask that "words are given" as we go.

Be the Word They Need

Be the Word. Say the words that are needed in the lives of those He puts in your path. Since the sword IS the Word, and the Word is what you believe and therefore a part of your shield, the actual words you say can be the words you say to yourself and to satan when the lying arrows are headed your way. The people you talk to probably have many arrows still flaming in their spiritual flesh. They feel defeated, rattled, put down—just like you've felt.

But, you have an answer. Boldly proclaim that. Speak truth lovingly into people's lives.

Here is a real-world example. I am currently talking to a guy about an hour a week. He has had some real issues in his life. He currently does not know Christ as his Lord. He has not believed in his heart that God raised Him from the dead, and he has not said with his mouth that Jesus is Lord. So, he currently is not saved. He admits it. So, he is under great shame right now and believing his dad's words toward him as a young boy. And yet, he is trying to figure out how to build armor without Christ—something that can't be done.

He says he can't accept Christ because Christ will not accept him. He is believing a big lie with all his heart. Where did he get those lies? From his dad's statements. Things like:

268 • *Tiny Armor?*

- "You can't get anything right!"
- "Why can't you do what I tell you?"
- "Are you an idiot? Why would you think that is a good idea?"
- "You are going to amount to nothing!"
- "Are ya stupid?"

As he told me these things, I said, "It seems like you feel condemned." He said, "All day, every day."

I said, "But you don't have to." He said, "But I do!"

As we were talking about the lies of the arrows, and that sometimes they come in groups, he said, "They are coming on so fast I can't stop a one of them." I said, "You have no shield."

He said, "I know."

At that moment, he knew that the only covering he had was from me and some other friends who were praying for him, encouraging him, and telling him about how we used to feel condemned so much. I still do at times, but not nearly like it was years ago. That is because I'm building my shield. We spent quite a bit of time talking about condemnation that comes in with *the tapes* of his dad's words. We talked about Romans 8:1 (which is a major piece on my shield): "There is therefore now *no condemnation* for those who are in Christ Jesus" (emphasis mine).

When the enemy shoots a lie at me, trying to tell me I'm worthless and therefore condemned, I tell him, "Not true.

I have great worth, and I am not condemned because I am in Christ Jesus, so back off."

But this guy knows that right now he is living under condemnation, and he feels the immense weight of it all. We also talked about the fact that he knows John 3:16 well—he just doesn't *believe* it yet for himself. He quoted it to me.

I then asked him if he knew the next couple verses, John 3:17–18.

He said, "No."

So, I told him with my *words,* "For God did not send his Son into the world to condemn the world, but in order that the world might be saved through him. Whoever believes in him is not condemned, but whoever does not believe is condemned already, because he has not believed in the name of the only Son of God." I continued, "This is why you feel the way you do. But you don't have to."

He said, "You don't understand. He cannot accept me. I have done too much."

He said he had to go, but we would talk again next week.

Here's another example. In 2 Corinthians 1:3–5, Paul says:

> *Blessed be the God and Father of our Lord Jesus Christ, the Father of mercies and God of all comfort, who comforts us in all our affliction, so that we may be able to comfort those who are in any affliction, with the comfort with which we ourselves are comforted by God. For as we share*

*abundantly in Christ's sufferings, so through
Christ we share abundantly in comfort too.*

Hand off some comfort to those you meet. The same comfort from God you used to build a part of your shield when satan lied to you and said, "God really doesn't care for you. He thinks you are worthless." You said, "No, He loves me, and He comforted me when I was going through some crap you initiated."

You need to change the pronouns and tell someone else that God can and will comfort them. But they must look to Him for that comfort when they are afflicted. When you talk that way to others, that's proclaiming who He is in your life, and who He could be in theirs. When you talk to someone you know who needs His words, don't default to sports, weather, and politics:

- Say things that matter to their soul.
- Say His words you know, because you have experienced them as you built your armor.
- Be bold.
- Cause a problem in hell.

From the moment we wake, the enemy does not want us proclaiming anything about God in any way. He will come after us even in our dreams. He does not care whether you are awake or asleep. In fact, last night I had some disturbing dreams. As I woke, I remembered them. I thought about them. It was not good. Not long after that it hit me: put your shield up and move forward with your sword! How easily I forget.

The prayers *(words)* of a righteous person, positionally and in actuality, are amazing! In James 5:16, God says, "The prayer of a righteous person has great power as it is working."

No prayer, no power.

We need power to go forth boldly. We pray for ourselves and for others. We pray for each other that the armor will hold, and we can move forward with the Word.

You can ask the Father before you close your eyes at bedtime to guard your thoughts and dreams during the night.

So much can happen in the first waking hours, and in the dreams the enemy will plant or use. When I was on staff at First Orlando, Pastor Jim Henry was teaching on prayer. I remember very clearly one thing he said:

You can ask the Father before you close your eyes at bedtime to guard your thoughts and dreams during the night.

The One who guards you during the day can do so at night. He never sleeps. He never stops caring about His children.

I had never really thought much about who initiated dreams. I always thought it was just the brain getting rid of old files, throwing them out as trash. And it was always jumbled up in a weird way. Like shred day at your local bank.

But sometimes, dreams are horrible. Nightmares! You can wake and actually remember terrifying actions, thoughts, deeds that you did, or what happened to you. I never knew that before I sleep, I can thank Him that He can and will be my armor covering while I sleep. Then He reminds me of the armor as soon as I wake, to put it on. Fight against the dreams, then move forward. God is for us. He loves us as His children.

He wants us equipped with armor, moving forward from the moment we wake until we sleep again. We're on the offense when we hold up the shield and the sword. So, what is it that we do when we move forward? Proclaim and declare as we run toward the gates of hell, toward the battle.

The Gates of Hell

Here is what it looks like in my mind's eye when I think about approaching the gates of hell. As I move forward, I will be taking territory which currently belongs to the enemy. The territory is the lives and souls of those he has imprisoned here on earth.

They are currently either:

- property of the enemy, as in not related to Christ yet, or,
- believers who have serious "spiritual strongholds" in their lives.

They are chained near the gates.

You may fall into one of those two categories. If so, we hope this has helped you. If you are not in one of those two categories, we pray as Paul asked us to, that you will *boldly* move toward those who are captive or have strongholds. You know some people who are having rough times. You know some people who have huge strongholds. You know some people who do not believe God is a loving God, or His Son, Christ, is a loving Savior who will accept them. As we pray for boldness in our lives, it is not just for our boldness. It is to use our words boldly. Not to be fearful.

Gates only prevail when we don't push against them.

When we commit to asking God for opportunity in the lives of others, we will invariably be moving toward the property line of hell. The fence line where satan hangs warning signs. He does not want you talking to or messing with anyone he has captive in any way. But our job is to walk up to that fence line, or gate, and poke the sword through it. He has to back up. Again, Jesus's brother, James, recorded this: "Resist the devil, and he will flee from you. Draw near to God, and he will draw near to you" (Jas. 4:7b–8a). But the enemy will fight us to keep us from moving forward toward others until he realizes he is required to back off. Do you believe that to be true? That with the Word of God which you have, you can resist the devil, and he is *required* to flee. Again, the armor is not only to defend. So, let's move forward. Let's cause a problem in hell.

———————————

Gates only prevail when we

don't push against them.

———————————

The Battle – Resist and He Will Flee

The apostle Paul was arguably the most heavily armored human in the New Testament. He believed Christ explicitly. He went places and did things that most of us get weak in the knees just thinking about. We may be scared to be nice to a neighbor because it may cost us more time than we think we have. Paul walked back into cities where they kicked him out, stoned him, and left him for dead. I'm not trying to shame you here. But God said through Paul, "Be imitators of me, as I am of Christ" (1 Cor. 11:1). Basically, Paul said, "Follow me as I follow Christ."

We can surely begin to ask God for the same boldness to use the armor well.

Is it scary?

Sometimes.

Is it right?

Always.

Remember, the word "resist" really means to "resist, stand firm, withstand," and how we do that while in battle determines the outcome. "Resist him, firm in your faith, knowing that the same kinds of suffering are being experienced by your brotherhood throughout the world" (1 Pet. 5:9).

"Therefore, take up the whole armor of God, that you may be able to *withstand* in the evil day…" (Eph. 6:13, emphasis mine). Again, the word for "withstand" is the same Greek word James uses as he wrote, "Resist the devil, and he will flee" (Jas. 4:7b). If you build armor and wear it, and show up ready not only to stand your ground, but also to help others, he is required to move back, to flee. But don't get puffed up—he is fleeing because of Christ, not because of you. Be immovable as you move forward always, not only at special times.

You want to know what the gates of hell look like? It looks like a little town in Central Mexico. Earlier in the book you read about an organization called G300. At an annual G300 dinner we had a young director from this town in Mexico speak about the impact the church was making in that little community which is overrun with gunfire as three separate drug cartels battle to overtake the area. The mayhem the citizens are subjected to is shocking, especially by U.S. standards. We will save you the drama and just say no one is safe there. But this young man's calling is to try to step into the lives of young children and teenagers who have a future with the cartel unless they can get some skills that will allow them to leave that area—if they survive that long.

One inspiring story is how his church just planted another church in the middle of this neighborhood, as a safe place for these young people and their parents. The pastor used to be a gang member. It's a major push against the gates of hell to boldly enter this area amidst unspeakable mayhem and build a church that can be a sanctuary for the community in the name of Christ.

I'll spare you the specifics, but let me give you one little peek at what he sees. When young people go missing, which happens all the time as collateral damage in a war zone, they often show back up in ice chests left on the road. You get the idea. It's horrible! The gates of hell—the teeth of satan taking on the entire community. And they have intentionally planted this church in the midst of the gunfire for Christ's sake. It kind of changes your perspective on how bad your day was. I think this is about as close to literally pushing back on the gates of hell as you can get. But you have your own gates to push against. Odds are your life is not quite that horrific. But there is an equivalent first-world situation for you. It probably doesn't involve your life being in danger. But your gates are the gates you are to push against.

Let's step back a moment as that concept sinks in: "risking yourself for other people." What does that look like in your life? It probably does not involve ice chests. Compare for a moment the difficulties of your situation and that situation. Your world and the one described above probably sound pretty different. You probably don't face a situation anywhere close to this one, so why are you worried? I understand your concern about embarrassment, rejection, losing a job, or having family turn on you if you step out and proclaim Christ to people around you. But, by comparison, are those big consequences compared to the leader in this story? If you help save someone from a bad eternity because you're willing to say something in love that might have the potential to cause you to have a really rough time for a moment, is that the right tradeoff?

The guy who ministers to those kids in Mexico everyday wouldn't ask for your pity. Your prayers, absolutely. He is counting on God protecting him and the kids as they grow. The key question is, are you looking for things in your life you can use to push against the gates of hell?

> *There is no such thing as "dress armor," only battle armor.*

I'm pretty sure the Holy Spirit has some ideas for you if you're asking Him for them. And I encourage you to ask Him. He has promised to lay the groundwork ahead of you, to protect you, to fund you, and to give you His power, and the words you need, when you need them. So, what are you waiting for?

As I have followed Christ, I have seen how He dealt with and still deals with the enemy. I look at the character of Christ and see how He acted. Since He IS the armor, how did He treat the enemy and how did He treat people? I see very little wrath. Yes, there is some righteous indignation when He turned over the tables and made the whip to drive out those selling in the temple. But I know He and the Trinity are One and have the same characteristics. I just see very little wrath in Christ. But, as I thought about this and asked God, I sensed this.

I asked God, "Why do I see so little wrath in Christ?"

In my imagination, I sensed Jesus look at God the Father, then look at God the Spirit, then back at me, and say in a very focused tone, "Oh, we're not done yet. Have you read Revelation?"

Jesus gave us Himself, who IS the armor, during His time on earth. There is a time coming when the enemy will be

There is no such thing as

"dress armor,"

only battle armor.

vanquished forever. We will not need the armor in heaven. Until then, as we live on this fallen planet, the battle ensues. Christ spent His time here defending, and rescuing. He gives us His armor and the same opportunities to defend and rescue. Wrath will come later. For now, armor up!

Pearly Gates

When you do show up at the pearly gates after your death, do not show up wearing shiny, tiny armor. That would only be proof that you never prepared for or engaged in battle for His sake. Show up battle-weary and battle-worn—and personally meet the Armor Himself.

Conclusion

We started with good news and bad news.

We end the same way.

Hopefully, you now see the context of the bad news, and are more aware of what satan is trying to do in all our lives. Often, the things that satan uses against us, we've provided him the raw material. The state of our hearts and our minds many times may make his attacks easy.

But we also hope you are much more aware of the good news of what God has planned for you. We are all on different journeys. We are at different levels of maturity and development in our walks with Him. Some people know more Scripture than others. Some are just getting started in their walk. You can't change where you are now. You are where you are. But, whether you stay there, or move forward fiercely determined to listen to the leadings of the Holy Spirit, you can get as much of Jesus as you want.

Hopefully, you give Him as much of you as you can. He wants nothing more than an intimate relationship with you, and that you grow to look more like Him. He wants that more than anything. Remember, you need to ask Him to enable your heart and mind to want to know Him better.

It's key. He knows how He created you, so He knows how you operate best. He knows your strengths and weaknesses and wants to help you with both. He wants you to have life and have it more abundantly. As with salvation, He does the major work of sanctification in our lives. But we have to lean in and cooperate with the changes and improvements He wants to make in us.

The result is a stronger, more effective soldier in His army that is trying to impact the world in His name. He wants to make us a more resilient warrior that walks boldly into the world in which we live so we can be the salt and light He wants us to bring to our families, friends, coworkers, neighbors, fellow Christians, and those who don't know the freedom of accepting His free gift of salvation. He made us for this journey. He enables us in it. He uses His words in Scripture and our prayers with Him to sharpen us, and to sharpen those around us. That is what makes this journey of life more abundant.

He wants us to layer on His Word to build us up. He wants us to pray with power and conviction. He wants to equip us to take on the gates of hell, whatever that looks like in our lives. He gives us the desire for all this, and enables our growth to look more like Him. It's an exciting journey and He's ready to take you from where you are now to wherever He wants you to be. You will be able to minister even better all along the way as you grow. When it's all over, He wants to continue that relationship in heaven forever. And, because of your obedience, you will hear the Armor Himself say, "Well done, good and faithful servant."

About the Authors
Doug Dees & Mark Lambert

For many years, in churches of all sizes from Arkansas to Oklahoma to Orlando, **Doug Dees** was the guy who helped people become followers of Christ, and disciple-makers. He sensed God saying he was to "proclaim the Word." He kept thinking that might mean to preach. But at the start of the fourth quarter of his life, he's realized very clearly that God is now saying to "proclaim from the housetops" through writing and blogging. His deepest desire is to help people know and love God more deeply, to look more like Christ...and to be led by the Spirit to help others do the same.

Doug was born and raised in Ft. Worth, Texas. He has degrees from Texas Wesleyan University, Southwestern Baptist Theological Seminary, and a doctorate from Reformed

Theological Seminary. He is married to Karen, the love of his life. They have two adult kiddos—Katie and Matt.

Mark Lambert is also a Ft. Worth native. He's been married for over forty-one years to his wife Melody. They have two married daughters, Ashlea and Lauren, and three grandkids. His grandson has a superman costume that matches his grandad's, and they wear them whenever the grandson wants.

Mark grew up in a close Christian family. He attended Southern Nazarene University. He's recently retired after working forty years, the last thirty-two of which were in the aerospace industry where he led cross-functional teams to achieve enterprise-wide improvements.

He enjoys hiking the twenty-four miles of the Grand Canyon in one long day. He has completed that trip seven times, two of which were with Doug. Mark meets with men's groups, or groups of men, for breakfast seven days a week. In case you think that's possible only because he's retired … he was meeting with five groups while he was working. He loves helping people to see God more clearly.

If you enjoyed this book, will you help us spread the word?

There are several ways you can help me get the word out about the message of this book...

- Post a 5-Star review on Amazon.
- Write about the book on your Facebook, Twitter, Instagram, LinkedIn – any social media you regularly use!
- If you blog, consider referencing the book, or publishing an excerpt from the book with a link back to my website. You have my permission to do this as long as you provide proper credit and backlinks.
- Recommend the book to friends – word-of-mouth is still the most effective form of advertising.
- Purchase additional copies to give away as gifts.

The best way to connect with me is by email:
dougjdees@gmail.com

Enjoy These Other Books by Doug Dees & Mark Lambert

You can order these books from Amazon and Barnes & Noble or where ever you purchase your favorite books.

Fish Prison
Doug Dees

Are you stuck? Is it possible that the rituals of work, and even church, may be keeping you confined and empty, instead of released and full? Yes, it is possible, but it' s also possible for you to become all of who God intends you to be, with freedom and purpose. The " Three Questions" in *Fish Prison* will help you live "beyond the glass" of confinement. But do understand that all three must be sincerely asked of God, all three of Him ... the Trinity. What could it hurt to ask Them?

How God Asks You to Love Others
A Field Guide

Mark Lambert & Doug Dees

This book is all about you learning to distin- guish your voice from God's, so that you can respond immediately when He taps you on the shoulder to do whatever He wants you to do in any of the relationships in your life. We are called to impart to the world around us. Are we ready to be a part of what He wants to do?

reSymbol
A Guide to reThink, reDefine, and reLease the Church

Doug Dees

When you think of church what comes to mind? A steeple? A cross? The unkind reality is this: the way we are thinking about church and operating church is not working as effectively as it could. *reSymbol* exposes some of the symbols that are competing with the visible Christ.

www.ingramcontent.com/pod-product-compliance
Lightning Source LLC
Chambersburg PA
CBHW071143130626
46553CB00004B/1496